# TESLA

## MODEL S

# BEST CAR EVER!

Frank van Gilluwe

Kim Rogers

Published by FAQware

## Acknowledgments

We thank Tesla Motors and the entire Tesla Motors team for producing such a great car. We also thank our family and friends for putting up with all our Tesla talk for years!

Design and Layout: Frank van Gilluwe

Library of Congress Control Number:  2013951866

ISBN 978-0-9860689-0-4
629.2293

Printed in the United States
10  9  8  7  6  5  4  3  2  1

## FAQware

PO Box 4434, Mountain View, CA 94040  USA
tms2014@faqware.com

www.FAQware.com  •  TelsaTap.com

# Table of Contents

Introduction

# Starting Up

Is the Tesla Model S the *best car ever*? If you're already an owner, then you know it's true. For the curious and the skeptics, I'm going to introduce you to the Model S and show you why it is the best car ever. And for you Model S owners, you'll learn even more about your fantastic car.

'Best car ever' is quite a boast. You'll find the Model S a revolutionary vehicle unlike anything before. It has it all – sex appeal, comfort, sports car handling, safety, style, powerful acceleration, extra passenger and cargo space, and much more. It even costs far less to run than the latest high-mileage hybrids and diesels. You'll never have to visit a gas station again.

Today, there are hundreds of cars to choose from. We'll explore why the Model S should be at the top of your list when considering any new car purchase.

**"Oh you're gonna drive an electric car, you just don't know it yet."** - *The Lefsetz Letter*

Now, be prepared to be surprised and delighted, as the Model S breaks so many illusions about what a car and a car company should be. It delivers what other car makers only dream about – an economical to run, environmentally friendly, stunningly fun-to-drive car that looks and performs great both inside and out!

## Common Terms

- EV - Electric Vehicle
- ICE - Internal Combustion Engine
- kWh - 1,000 Watts per hour of electricity
- MPG - Miles Per Gallon

# How I Discovered the Model S

I'm an entrepreneur, writer and car enthusiast. I've owned a number of great vehicles from sporty cars like the Acura NSX to top of the line luxury cars from Audi and Lexus. When choosing a car, safety and reliability are top priorities, but I also prefer a car with great style, comfort and design. Until Tesla came along, I've liked my cars but never loved one until I bought the Tesla Model S.

As an electronics engineer, I've always understood the advantages of electric vehicles. I even looked into making one myself. As luck would have it, Tesla Motors came along and started showing off the Roadster, an electric sports car. I liked the entire concept and began following Tesla closely. When I got a chance to see the Roadster prototype in person, I jumped at the chance. Such a cool car, but being a very low car, it was challenging getting in and out. I was just getting too old to do this anymore, and that was one of the reasons I parted with my fun NSX.

Fortunately, Tesla was also designing a follow-on sports sedan to the Roadster, the Model S. I was invited to the first public unveiling of this all-electric sedan at Menlo Park, California in March 2009. At the time, there was very little known about this sports sedan, so I was not expecting anything really significant. Wow, was I wrong! Tesla gave everyone a short, exhilarating drive around the parking lot. To understand how monumental that was, prototypes cost millions of dollars to make. Most manufacturers do not let anyone sit in one, let alone take passengers for a drive. This prototype sedan looked and felt like a production ready car. I was sold and made my reservation a couple of days later.

**Cool Fact**

While waiting for the Models S, Tesla sent the early reservation holders a nice gift – a remote controlled toy Roadster!

There are some who might think I was crazy to believe in Tesla. After all, Tesla had not yet delivered a single car to a customer and the Model S used all sorts of new technologies. Yet, I recognized the genius in its simple and elegant design. I knew this was the start of something entirely new and exciting, and I wanted to be a part of it.

While waiting for my car to be delivered, I continued to follow Tesla closely, and even created the TeslaTap.com fan website. After waiting almost four years, I received my Model S in January 2013. Wow, it was worth the wait!

Obviously I'm impressed with both the car and the company. So much so, I spent a half-year writing this book. Now that's crazy! Having closely watched Tesla through the start of the Model S to now being an owner, I'll guide you through everything you want to know about the Model S!

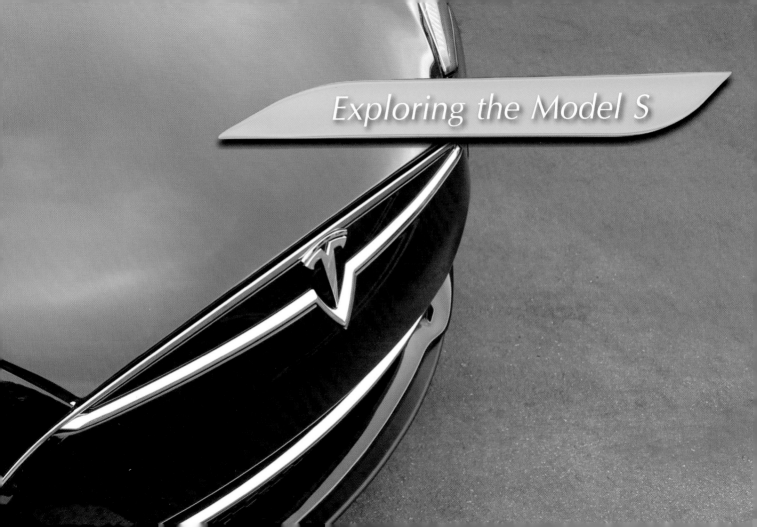

Exploring the Model S

# High Style

Tesla's Model S has proven that environmentally friendly cars do not have to be econoboxes, but can be roomy, luxurious, and high performance. Franz von Holzhausen, the chief designer of the Model S, delivered a stunningly great car that turns heads and won numerous design awards.

Starting from a clean slate, the exterior delivers an elegant refined style, reminiscent of Aston Martin but with distinct features maximized for superior aerodynamics. The most notable are the retractable door handles that slide out when approaching the car.

*Franz von Holzhausen*

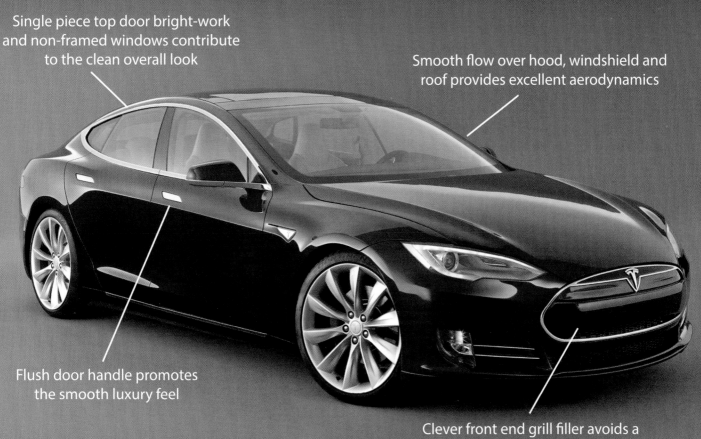

Single piece top door bright-work and non-framed windows contribute to the clean overall look

Smooth flow over hood, windshield and roof provides excellent aerodynamics

Flush door handle promotes the smooth luxury feel

Clever front end grill filler avoids a common style mistake often made on other electric vehicles

The aerodynamic styling also delivers an incredibly low drag coefficient of .24, the lowest for any production car in 2012. As comparison for other cars in 2012, consider that one of the world's fastest production cars, the Ferrari 458 Italia has a drag coefficient of .33 while the Mini Cooper, a car half the size of the Model S has a .35 drag coefficient rating. Reducing the drag increases the car's range and makes for a quiet car!

Another exterior design feature that stands out as being first of its kind is the optional all-glass panoramic roof. The rear glass panel is fixed, and the front glass panel is fully adjustable. It also includes a pop-up mesh panel to prevent wind buffeting when open.

Franz von Holzhausen made the wise decision to make the Model S look "timelessly modern" with a futuristic hint yet familiarity of a classic car. The Model S proves conclusively that electric cars do not need to look ugly or boring.

"**The Model S got its roots from the idea of being not only the best electric car, but the best performance sedan in the marketplace**"

*- Franz von Holzhausen*

### Cool Fact

Prior to Tesla, Franz von Holzhausen was responsible for the design of a number of cars including the Mazda RX-8, Pontiac Solstice and Saturn Sky.

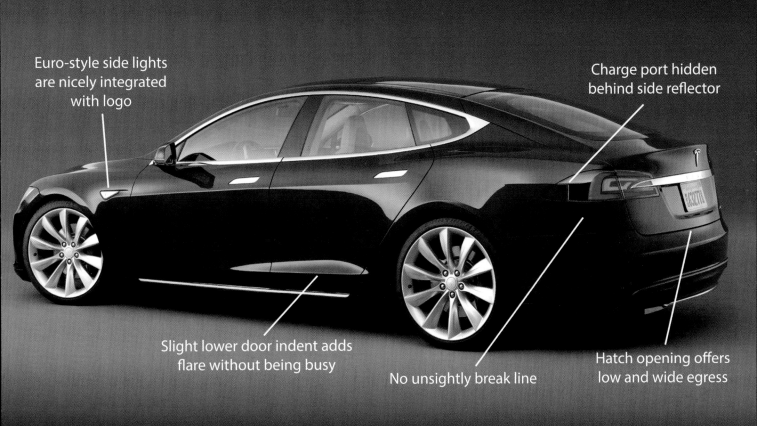

Euro-style side lights are nicely integrated with logo

Charge port hidden behind side reflector

Slight lower door indent adds flare without being busy

No unsightly break line

Hatch opening offers low and wide egress

The interior design takes full advantage of the flat floor to provide a very spacious feeling. The extra width of the car and lack of a center hump means the rear seat comfortably seats three adults with plenty of legroom.

The most distinctive feature of the interior is the 17" touch screen display placed conveniently between the driver and front seat passenger. This is the command center of the vehicle and the central focus of the interior.

The dashboard and cup holder areas are trimmed with a choice of lacewood or obeche wood veneers, a high-gloss piano black, or carbon fiber.

Another outstanding feature of the Model S is its interior configurability. While many like the minimalistic design, Tesla offers a center console insert for those that want a more conventional layout for extra storage and additional cup holders. An optional rear facing third seat is big enough for two small children or fold down both back seats to get more cargo space.

**Cool Fact**

Obeche wood comes from a tropical tree in Africa and offers unusually low heat retention.

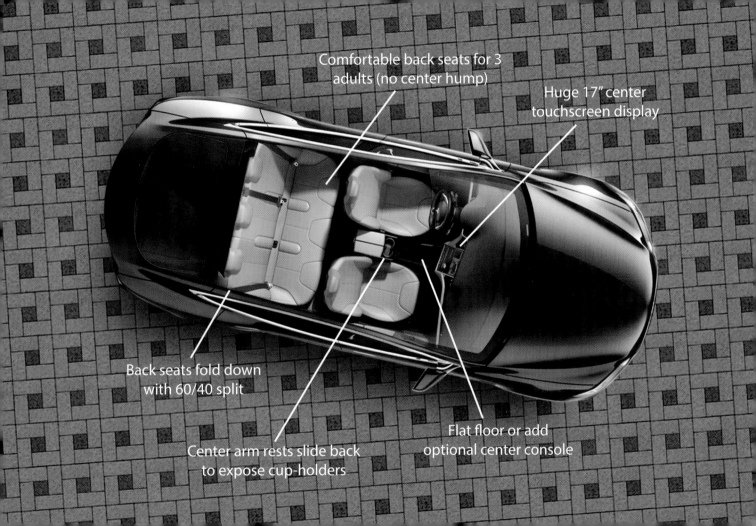

Comfortable back seats for 3 adults (no center hump)

Huge 17" center touchscreen display

Back seats fold down with 60/40 split

Center arm rests slide back to expose cup-holders

Flat floor or add optional center console

# Space to Spare

The Model S has an unusually large amount of cargo space, exceeding most large sedans and SUVs! With the battery and motor in the floor, it opens up both the front and rear for storage. Under the hood is a five cubic feet area that is big enough for luggage or ideal for anything you wish to hide. No other luxury car has this extra storage compartment. Tesla likes to call this a *frunk* as it's a trunk in the front.

Behind the rear seat is a 26 cubic feet area for additional storage. This includes a hidden well at the very back of the car. The cargo space behind the rear seats exceeds many other cars and SUVs, like the 2014 BMW X5 which has about 24 cubic feet, or a 2014 Acura MDX that only has about 16 cubic feet.

The Model S comes with 60/40 split-folding rear seats. Fold the rear seats down in the Model S and this space increases to 58 cubic feet! Furthermore, the hatchback door makes accessing this huge rear storage so much easier than most sedans.

Both the rear liftgate and the frunk hood are electrically released with the FOB or from the control panel in the car. The optional tech package includes a power liftgate that opens and closes at the press of a button.

# Take a Seat

Here again Tesla surprised everyone by designing the first sports sedan with seating for seven. The Model S achieves this with an optional three-row seating arrangement without compromising its wonderfully sleek exterior look or losing all its trunk space. Most drivers opt for the base model which seats five adults quite comfortably.

Seats come standard in black cloth with synthetic leather trim, or optional Nappa leather in black, gray or tan. Signature editions have the choice of Nappa white leather. Front seats include 12-way power adjustments and heated seats. With the tech package, the driver seat includes multiple memory profiles.

Besides the two front seats, the second row holds three additional adults. Cars with the optional cold weather package also get three-zone heated second row seats. The rear seats fold down in a 60/40 split if additional cargo space is needed.

In an ICE car, a person must straddle a large floor hump when sitting in the center back seat. This seat is also more uncomfortable because there's less padding due to the hump. This is not a problem in a Model S. With its flat floor, the Model S gives all three adults proper leg room and fully padded seats.

> ### Cool Fact
> Cars equipped with the panoramic roof get an additional 1.5 inches (4 cm) of front and rear seat headroom.

*Grey Leather Interior*

17

The Model S also has an option for rear-facing child seats accessible from its hatchback door. Each seat comes with a five-point seat belt for safety. This optional third-row "jump seat" is designed for two children between 35 and 77 pounds, and at least 37 inches or 93 cm tall. When not in use, the seat assembly folds out of the way into the bottom well, maintaining a flat rear deck for cargo. Adding this rear-facing seat still leaves the owner with the frunk, the front trunk space.

The Model S performs and looks like a sports car yet fits the passenger needs of a family car.

### Safety Fact

When building the Model S for the optional third row seats, Tesla installs a second bumper. This provides additional protection in the event of a rear end collision. The third row is also the safest location in the car for front and side impacts.

# Let There Be Light

Tesla's exterior lighting delivers excellent illumination and signaling functionality in a uniquely stylish way. As you would expect of a luxury forward-thinking car, Tesla makes extensive use of LED lighting throughout the Model S. LED lighting has many advantages. Compared with incandescent bulbs, they are far cooler to the touch, use considerably less power and should last the lifetime of the car.

Starting from the front, we see the distinctive LED daytime running lights that surround the projector headlights. High-Intensity Discharge (HID) Xenon headlights are now standard equipment. An additional amber LED turn signal strip is integrated into the assembly. Immediately below are optional cornering lights, amber side marker lights and optional fog lights.

Side lights are required in some European countries, but are rarely seen on cars in North America. On each side of the Model S are backlit side turn signals with the Tesla logo. These side turn signals increase the visibility of this car while also adding to its distinctive look.

Another unique lighting feature is seen when the door handle extends out. A light illuminates below the handle towards the ground. When the door opens a second light on the underside of the door illuminates to show the way. The red safety reflector on the door is illuminated when any door is open. Some of these lights are only included with the Tech Package or Premium Interior Lighting options.

On the back of the Model S are the taillights, backup lights, rear side reflex lights and license plate lights. LED taillights improve safety as it's estimated the brake lights come on far quicker than conventional taillights. At 60 mph, it may give a driver an extra warning of 15 feet of travel time. A very wide, 44 LED, center stop light stretches across the top of the liftgate for even more visibility.

While European versions are equipped with amber rear turn signal lights, the Model S in the United States has red lights. This is due to the Department of Transportation regulatory requirements for the amount of surface area for rear turn lights. These regulations were written before the advent of LEDs and are difficult if not impossible to change. To meet these requirements with the current taillight design, both the rear outside brake light and turn signal light blink together in US versions of the car and must be red.

*Amber rear turn signal light for European cars*

The interior lighting is understated and in keeping with the sleek, sexy design of the Tesla Model S.

All four primary passenger positions get individual task lights for reading and both front passengers get puddle lights when the doors are open.

Although there are far fewer buttons in the Model S than other vehicles, they are all back-lit at night. This includes the buttons on the steering wheel, window controls, mirror adjustments, emergency flashers, and the glove-box release.

The Premium Interior Lighting option adds accent lighting throughout the cabin. This includes lights for the front footwells, lights for the rear floor, a strip of lights on each of the doors and rear door puddle lights. All these lights are unobtrusive, but provide a comfortable ambient glow at night.

Like other luxury cars, the interior lights automatically come on when the driver approaches and goes off when the driver walks away. Additional lighting is provided in both the front and rear trunk areas when open and the glove box interior.

*Glove box release button*

**Cool Fact**

The Premium Interior Lighting option adds about 60 LEDs throughout the cabin.

*Inside Door Accent Light*

# Flying Colors

Tesla offers the Model S in nine attractive exterior body colors. The car's base price includes a choice between a solid black or white exterior. The other seven color options cost extra. They include five metallic colors, a multi-coat pearl white and multi-coat red. Signature red metallic is an exclusive color for the first group of Model S Signature editions released in each region.

To meet its exceptional high quality standards, Tesla employs a sophisticated paint system to paint each car. The process begins by dunking the aluminum body in a pre-treatment bath and then an electro-coating bath. The electro-coating is then baked on to protect against corrosion. Next, a sealer is applied for waterproofing. Each car gets a primer coat, a color coat, and a final clear coat all done by robotic arms to ensure absolute uniformity. Cars with multi-coat colors get a second color coat to increase the color depth.

Tesla offers a paint armor option for improved protection from debris, stones, bugs, and weathering on key areas. Paint armor is a heavy clear film that is best applied when the car is new and the paint is in perfect condition.

## Cool Fact

About ten Signature customers talked Tesla into painting their cars with custom colors in 2012. Tesla charged an extra $12,000 for custom paint jobs. At the time, Tesla found it was more difficult and time consuming than it was worth and discontinued the option.

Solid White     Silver     Grey     Signature Red     Red

Green     Blue     Solid Black     Brown     Pearl White

# Wheels in Motion

Tesla offers 19 and 21 inch aluminum rims and tire combinations to meet appearance and driving preferences. All deliver a comfortable, quiet ride.

The Model S includes 19 inch Goodyear Eagle RS-A2 high performance all-season tires. Optional 19 inch Michelin Primacy tires improve range by three percent. The 21 inch Continental ExtremeContact tires are another option. The Performance Plus model comes with even higher-performance Michelin Pilot Sport PS2 tires that require 21" rims. This tire also improves range by two to five percent.

Depending on the tire size selected, alternative rims, such as the 19 inch Cyclone or 21 inch Turbine are available.

Tesla has offered a 19 inch Aerodynamic rim option in the past that provides an additional three percent range improvement, but was discontinued due to low demand.

Some customers prefer 21 inch tires for appearance, improved traction and handling. However, the trade off for using 21 inch tires is shorter tread life, less resistance to damage, and unsuitability for winter driving conditions.

Tesla does not include a spare tire or offer run flat tires for the Model S. They do offer several tires for different handling and climate conditions as well as snow chains. The 19 inch winter Pirelli 240 Sottozero tires are recommended for winter conditions.

If you change the tires yourself, the wheel lug nuts should be tightened to 129 lb/ft (175 N.m.) which is more than most cars.

**Standard**     **Cyclone**     **Aerodynamic**

*19"*

**Turbine**     **Turbine Gray**

*21"*

# Get in Touch

The huge 17" high-definition touchscreen is one of the standout features of the Model S that can't be missed. It's like an iPad™ except it's bigger and easier to use. Swiping, dragging to scroll, or pinching to zoom are pleasantly familiar to any smartphone or tablet user.

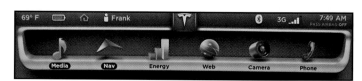

*Status and primary controls*

Tesla's screen layout is extremely intuitive. Key status indicators and controls are always present and never disappear. The common controls are accessed with a single tap. Sub-menus to access additional functions have been kept to a bare minimum. Compare this to layers of confusing, deeply nested menus seen so often on other cars.

The very top of the display shows status and less frequently used controls, such as: tapping the battery to get to the charging screen, Homelink to open a garage, driver profiles, Bluetooth setup, and WiFi setup.

**Hidden Secret**

Press both scroll wheels in and hold for fifteen seconds to reboot the main display. A reboot does not affect the ability to drive.

*Touchscreen with map and music selected*

In the main viewing area, you tap one of the large icons to view the media system, navigation, energy usage history graph, the web browser, a backup camera view, or the phone and contacts list. Select either a single full frame view or two different half-views. The Model S is the first car to provide a full Web browser accessible even when the car is in motion. Taking advantage of the split screen capability, a passenger could be viewing the Web for a restaurant while the driver is viewing the Google Map.

At the display bottom, tap CONTROLS for access to locks, lights and other details. See the next section for more on Controls. The volume control adjusts the current audio stream.

The climate status and choices are always available at the display bottom. See "Cabin Comfort" on page 36 for more details.

### Cool Facts
The display is full high-definition providing 1080 x 1920 resolution.

*Touchscreen with connected phone call and energy usage graph*

# In Control

In the lower left corner of the touchscreen, the **CONTROLS** button provides access to less frequently used vehicle controls and settings.

From the controls tab, change the sunroof, driving settings, view and clear trip counters, adjust the display brightness, manually activate the brake (it's automatically activated in Park), or power down the car.

Tap the **CHARGING** button to set the amount of charge and status. A GPS location-based start charging time takes advantage of lower-cost, late night power rates.

The *Doors & Locks* section shows the current status of the doors, frunk, rear liftgate and charge port. Lock or unlock doors, release the frunk hood, open and close the rear liftgate, or release the charge port door.

The *Lights* section controls the headlights, daytime running lights and dome light state. It also controls the fog and ambient lights if the car is so equipped. Many of the lights activate automatically, so this screen is rarely used.

### Cool Fact

The images of the car in the controls screen match the car's actual color, tire size and rims. If a specific light is on, it lights up on the car image as well!

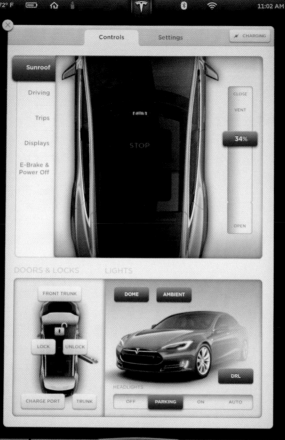

*Controls screen with sunroof, frunk, side door and rear liftgate shown open*

# Cabin Comfort

Tesla breaks new ground even with the climate system. When you approach the car and the door handles extend, the climate control system immediately starts up. Depending on the temperature setting, you quickly get a nice hot or cool breeze before you start off!

The climate control system uses a variable speed heat pump similar to that used in many homes. This latest technology is one of the most efficient means to deliver hot or cold air. Since there is no engine to warm up, it also works much faster than the conventional ICE car.

Climate controls are always available at the bottom of the 17" touchscreen. Controls include left and right cabin temperature, seat heaters, front and rear defrosters, climate power, and access to additional climate controls. The left temperature control also has an option to keep the left and right cabin temperature in sync or not.

Status appears in the upper center, including roughly how fast the fan is running, airflow direction, air-conditioning setting and circulation (*not shown*).

Tapping the CUSTOM option in the center allows you to set additional climate options (*right*).

In very hot climates the range may be reduced between five and ten percent when using A/C. With freezing conditions, owners see a range loss between 10 and 20 percent when using the heater. This is significantly better than the 50 percent range loss reported by some Chevy Volt and early Nissan Leaf owners.

For some, using the seat warmers may be a more efficient alternative to using the cabin heater. The optional Subzero Weather Package includes a three-zone rear seat warmer, which are activated from the CONTROLS button.

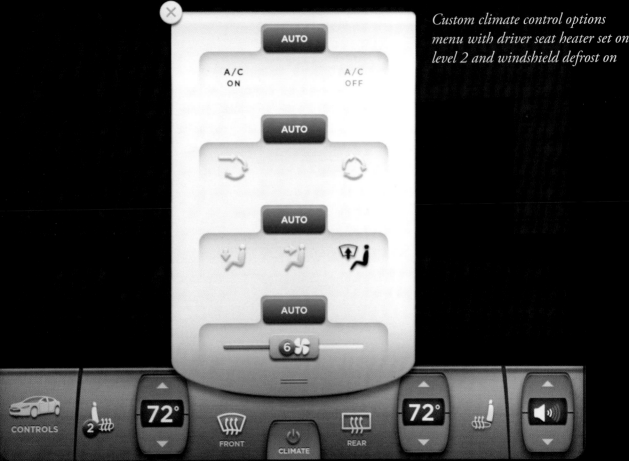

*Custom climate control options menu with driver seat heater set on level 2 and windshield defrost on*

# Finding Your Way

Here again, Tesla differentiates itself from other car manufacturers with two navigation views: Google Maps on the 17" touchscreen display and a Garmin navigation system on the left side of the instrument display. Navigation comes as part of the optional Tech package. But unlike most car manufacturers, Tesla's Tech package includes seven years of free Garmin map updates. In addition, the Google Maps on the Model S displays real-time traffic updates and displays topographic satellite images with overlaid roads.

Destinations are set from a voice command, selected from a prior address in history, from any previous location where you charged, or any supercharger location. Destinations are also set from a typed in address. As you type, Google automatically lists the most likely candidates before you complete typing – making it far less painful than other systems.

Once a destination is confirmed, the Google Map shows the path, while a smaller 3D guide map appears in the instrument display. This 3D map shows upcoming turns and events and follows your direction of travel. Its main advantage is that it is always available and doesn't require the wireless connectivity that Google Maps requires.

The 17" touchscreen display also shows the route of travel. The navigation dialog shows a list of the next upcoming turns, distances, estimated time remaining, and estimated time of arrival. Voice prompting is also available.

Like all current generation navigations systems, if you deviate from the recommended route, it automatically reroutes. Unlike other navigation systems, there is no need to periodically buy or install new maps. Any improvements Google makes to its maps are immediately available on the Model S.

*Instrument panel display (opposite page) and primary map display (above) are illustrative of two different destinations.*

# Music to My Ears

The audio system for the Model S offers a wide range of ways to get your music fix. This includes AM/FM/FM-HD and optional XM radios; streaming audio via TuneIn or Slacker over the built in 3G system; Bluetooth from your cell phone or other devices; or via files stored on a USB connected device.

With the large display and well-designed interface, it's easy to select the source, audio stations, album or a specific song. Alternatively, use the voice recognition system to select a song by saying "*Play Justin Timberlake Mirrors*". When songs are played, it automatically locates and displays the related cover art, a nice touch.

The volume is controlled on the display in any mode, but the left steering scroll wheel is easier to use for volume adjustment. Tap the scroll wheel to pause/mute the sound.

The Model S comes standard with a reasonable 7-speaker stereo. A 12-speaker Ultra High Fidelity Sound upgrade is available that includes a sub-woofer, larger amps, and XM radio, The upgrade also includes Dolby ProLogic IIx to convert stereo music content into 7.1 surround sound, but most owners prefer to leave this off.

## Cool Fact

For better music quality in any car, avoid streaming with Bluetooth from your phone. Bluetooth highly compresses the audio.

**Where The Road Will Lead Us**

Weekend in Monaco

Rippingtons

2:53                                    -1:22

# Instrument of Desire

Tesla is the first production car to use a high-resolution 12.3-inch LCD instrument panel that changes depending on the current state of the car and customer preferences. The instrument panel has all the typical indicators and much more.

The display is divided into four sections: left, center and right and top. When driving, the center of the display shows a large circular gauge with vehicle speed in both digital and analog forms, along with instantaneous power consumption/regeneration meters. Driving range appears based on the amount of battery power remaining and past usage patterns.

When the car is off, the speedometer/energy gauge is replaced with a view of the car showing the status of the doors and the driving range available.

To select content on the left and right displays, press the corresponding scroll wheel in for a couple of seconds and then scroll through the options. The left side selects between navigation, audio information, trip data, and an energy usage graph. The right side offers similar content selections, adds phone options, and the ability to adjust the fan speed, cabin temperature, display brightness and media source.

Along the top of the display are the typical status, warning and problem icons, like *headlights on* and *tire pressure low*. When needed additional text appears to explain what the warning means. All of these extra features and personalization make it the most informative instrument display on the market today.

*Instrument panel with navigation and energy graph*

# Remote Control

The Tesla mobile app provides remote control and tracking of your car through the built in 3G connection. Tesla makes the app available for free, in both Android and iPhone versions. A few technical savvy owners have also created versions for Windows phones (called Tesla Connect), and for BlackBerry phones (called Model S for BlackBerry).

Using the mobile app, you can check the car's current lock state, remotely lock or unlock the car, honk the horn or flash the lights – handy if you can't quite remember where your car is parked. If the car is equipped with the sunroof, vent or close the roof.

The mobile app is also useful for real-time monitoring of the charging status. When charging, it shows the current range; how many minutes remain until you reach your desired charge level and the charging rate. A button toggles the desired charge between Standard and Max Range. This is especially handy while charging at a Supercharger and running other errands.

Before you leave for your next destination, remotely set the cabin at your perfect temperature. It even shows the current cabin temperature.

In the location view, you can see where the car is at the moment, either with Google maps or a satellite view. The current speed is shown if the car is moving.

> **Cool Fact**
>
> Remotely preheat or cool your car with the app. If you don't access the car within 30 minutes, the climate control turns off automatically.

*Tesla mobile app screens*

# Silence is Golden

When the car turns on, the lack of engine noise is the first thing people notice. According to the Edmunds Test Track sound test, the Model S measures an exceptionally low 36.4 dB when stopped. The electric motor is completely silent.

Cabin noise generally comes from three sources: mechanical bits, wind and tires. Getting rid of all those noisy ICE parts such as the engine, transmission, belts, fuel pump and muffler dramatically reduce the Tesla cabin noise. With its class leading .24 coefficient of drag, wind noise is barely noticeable. The only noises you may hear are the tires on the pavement, and even those are nicely muted.

Most ICE vehicles seem quite noisy in comparison. Cranking the radio volume up may mask some of the noise, but that really just adds to the din. Continuous loud noise significantly reduces alertness, increasing the risk of an accident. If you are talking on the phone or with other passengers, it requires raising your voice to be heard.

On the outside, the Model S is definitely quieter than its ICE counterparts. While not really silent, the slight drivetrain whine and possibly the HVAC motor is heard if there are no other noises nearby. This requires a bit more caution by the Model S driver, as pedestrians and bicyclists may not be aware of your presence.

## Crazy Facts

Some BMW and Porsche models actually feed noise from the exhaust system back into the cabin. The latest Cadillac CTS plays recorded engine noises through the stereo!

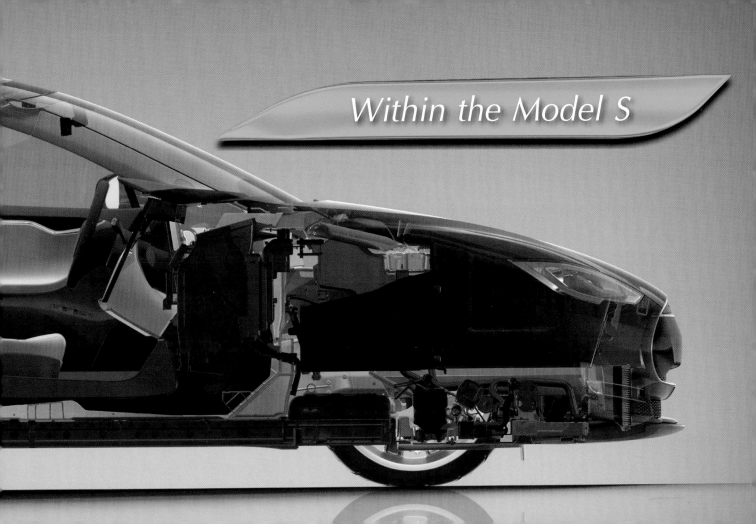

# Within the Model S

# Safety First

The Model S is one of the safest cars on the road. It was specifically designed to exceed conventional safety standards. As an EV, it offers safety advantages that no ICE car can claim. This extraordinary attention to safety was validated by the NHTSA. The Model S received a 5-star safety rating from NHTSA in every category. When the NHTSA conducted the Model S test, only 1% of the cars tested by the US government could achieve this high rating. This score reflects testing for front, side, and rear impacts as well as rollover events.

The car includes standard safety features expected in a luxury car and some unique ones that make this car even safer. It's often overlooked but the best safety system is one that avoids a crash in the first place! The superb driving experience of the Model S helps drivers avoid accidents with its combination of excellent handling, instant accelerator response and very low center of gravity. Other safety features include oversized brakes with ABS, traction control, stability control, tire pressure monitoring, rear view camera, and instant-on LED brake lights.

The Model S offers the latest occupant protection features with a total of eight airbags including front and side impact airbags, pelvis and knee airbags. The added stiffness and overall rigidity from the battery pack in the car floor increases occupant protection from side impacts. Front seat belt pretensioners are standard equipment.

Unlike conventional cars, the Model S has no engine in the front. In a serious front-end crash, there is always a risk that the ICE car engine is pushed into the lap of the passengers leading to serious if not fatal injuries. This can't happen in a Model S. Instead, safety is improved with unusually large crumple zones in the front and rear, due to the lack of a conventional engine and transmission.

*NHTSA Side-impact test gets a 5-star rating*

*NHTSA Front-impact test gets a 5-star rating*

This superior crumple zone design uses double-octagon extrusions to better protect the occupants. In the event of a head-on collision, this design reduces the impact to the opposing car and the large crumple zone benefits both parties. When a Model S is ordered with the optional 3rd row of seating, Tesla installs a second internal bumper for additional rear occupant protection.

*Firefighters practice forced door removal on a car donated by Tesla*

The Model S uses an aluminum body that is reinforced with high strength, boron steel with corrosion inhibitors. This avoids the rust and corrosion that weakens conventional steel and steel connection points over time. A steel car's crash energy absorption capabilities decline rapidly over time in wet and salty environments, while the Model S remains like new for the life of the car.

When all factors are equal and two vehicles collide, the heavier vehicle protects its occupants better than a lighter one. Even though the aluminum body on the Model S reduces weight, the batteries add back weight. The Model S ends up being similar in weight to other large luxury vehicles from BMW, Lexus, and Mercedes.

While many ICE cars offer the mandated minimum requirements, the Model S offers superior safety for you and your family.

### Cool Fact
The Model S roof crush resistance greatly exceeds federal requirements and broke a crush machine during testing!

# Safety Features

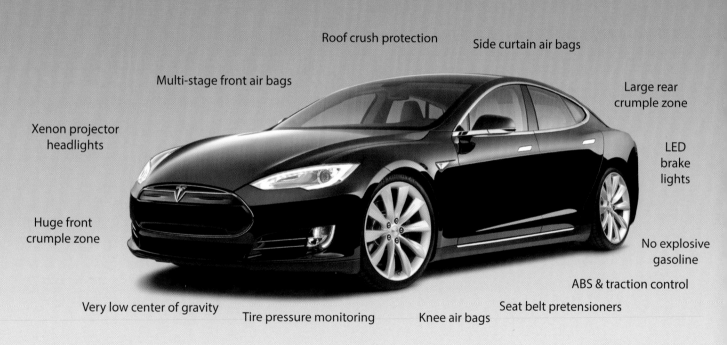

Roof crush protection

Side curtain air bags

Multi-stage front air bags

Large rear crumple zone

Xenon projector headlights

LED brake lights

Huge front crumple zone

No explosive gasoline

ABS & traction control

Very low center of gravity

Tire pressure monitoring

Knee air bags

Seat belt pretensioners

# Batteries Included

The battery pack is the core of the Model S and Tesla's most compelling invention. It provides a key competitive advantage over other battery systems. Tesla combines over 7000 lithium-Ion cells into a 4" thick battery pack. The battery pack includes an unusual number of active and passive safety systems. These include a heating and cooling system, individual battery fuses, separated cells to avoid a cascade effect if one cell were to fail, a smoke detection system and a disconnect system in the event of a serious impact.

The pack is comprised of 16 semi-independent modules that are monitored for health and control of the charging and discharging of the batteries.

Panasonic Corporation is the primary supplier of the 18650-form-factor 3.1Ah cells in Tesla's battery packs and was an early investor in Tesla. What makes these the most cost-efficient, reliable, custom designed cells is not its shape but its proprietary nickel-cobalt-aluminum lithium-ion chemical recipe inside.

The flat battery pack under the car floor offers three advantages: adds stiffness and a lower center of gravity for race-car like handling; improved interior space; and enables rapid battery pack swapping.

All this technology results in a very high-capacity system, that powers the car farther than any production electric car to date. The official EPA rating for the 60 kWh battery pack is a 208 mile range at 95 MPG-equivalent combined city and highway driving. The 85 kWh battery pack received an official EPA rating of 265 mile range at 89 MPG-equivalent combined city and highway driving.

The Panasonic batteries were designed for 3000 full charge cycles with minimal degradation. Using the smallest 60 kWh pack with its EPA rating of 208 miles a charge, this means 3000 times 208 for a life of 624,000 miles! Assuming the car is driven 12,000 miles a year for a lifetime of 624,000 miles, the battery pack could theoretically last 52 years. The larger pack has an even longer potential life. Even if other factors reduced this number by half, battery life concerns appear unwarranted. Tesla warrants the battery for 8 years and 125,000 miles (and unlimited miles for the 85 kWh editions), so few batteries will ever need to be replaced under warranty.

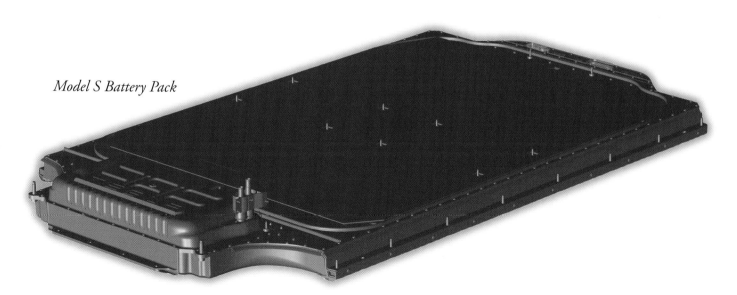

*Model S Battery Pack*

# Moving Forward

One of the beauties of a fully electric car is the simplicity of the powertrain. Tesla designed the motor in the Model S to have one moving part that should last the life of the car. The liquid-cooled, three-phase four-pole induction motor can run up to 16,000 RPM. The peak motor power ranges between 302 and 416 hp depending on the car model.

A single-speed transaxle with a 9.73-to-1 reduction drives the rear wheels through a traditional differential. There is no transmission, flywheel, starter or drive shaft. The entire Model S powertrain takes up less space than an automatic transmission! All this simplicity means higher reliability and considerably less maintenance costs since there's so little that can wear out or become defective.

When you step on the accelerator for an ICE car, you have to wait for the gas to start pumping; the turbo (if present) to spin up; the engine to overcome inertia of all those moving parts; the transmission's clutch to stop slipping, and wait for the effects of drivetrain lash-up to end. In stark contrast, the instant low-end torque of the Model S accelerates faster and far smoother than other cars. Tesla specifies the P85 edition with acceleration from 0 to 60 mph in 4.2 seconds. Motor Trend ran their own test in 2012 and did 0-60 mph in 3.9 seconds. The bottom line is that the Model S is wonderfully fast and does it all with quiet efficiency!

## Cool Fact

The motor requires no rare-earth magnets typically used in other electric cars and hybrids.

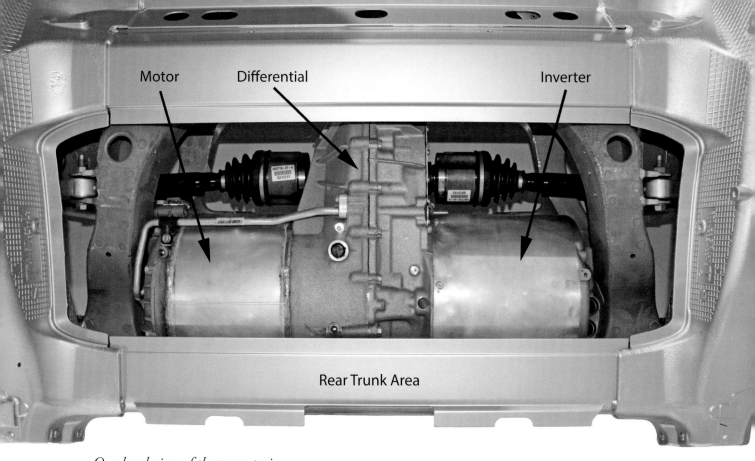

Motor    Differential    Inverter

Rear Trunk Area

*Overhead view of the powertrain*

# Get a Grip

## Traction Control

Traction control is a safety feature that keeps the driven wheels from losing grip. This helps avoid the vehicle spinning out under ice, mud, or other unusual surfaces. It also protects the tires from damage when the vehicle has more power than the tires have grip.

With conventional ICE cars that offer traction control, the application is quite crude. It typically involves reducing engine power by cutting off the fuel or stopping the spark to one or more cylinders. Due to the physical engine design with considerable mass in the drivetrain, the engine starts to slow down until traction control detects the return of proper grip. This means it's slow to react and can interfere with an expert driver's ability to control the car. For that reason, many cars include an option to reduce the onset of traction control. Still, it is often bet-

ter and safer for most users to keep traction control fully active.

With traction control completely disabled, some crazy vehicle owners like to do burnouts in a safe area like an unused, open parking lot. Applying more power to the wheels than the tires can grip, cause the tires to spin and

### Cool Fact

To do wild burnouts on the Model S, you'll have to remove the traction control fuse. This disables ABS, stability control, traction control along with stopping brake assist, the speedometer, air suspension, and power steering systems. Obviously, it's unsafe to drive in this condition!

smoke. Often a set of tires can be destroyed in a single burnout, so it could be quite expensive and could leave you stranded!

The Tesla Model S includes a superior traction control system. Since the control of the electric motor is almost instantaneous, traction control works unobtrusively, delivering the right amount of power at all times. This increases safety and stability even under heavy acceleration. The P85 Edition offers sport-tuned traction control which allows a little slip for high-performance drivers.

## Stability Control

When you enter a skid, such as on ice, the best advice is to steer into the skid and slow until the vehicle traction returns. While easier said than done, some vehicles such as SUVs are inherently unstable due to the high center of gravity that makes it difficult to control under skid conditions.

Electronic Stability Control (ECS) helps to keep a vehicle under control during a skid. This safety system works by comparing the direction of travel with the steering input. Normally, these vectors are the same. When the car skids, the vectors diverge and the ECS system applies specific brake pressure to one or more wheels. It may also reduce the engine/motor output. While it can't do miracles, it greatly improves handling under skid conditions.

The United States Insurance Institute for Highway Safety found that ECS equipped vehicles reduced the risks of multiple vehicle crashes by 32% and single vehicle crashes by 40%. This startling statistic likely led ESC to be required on all new cars sold in the USA since 2012. Of course, the Models S includes this valuable safety system.

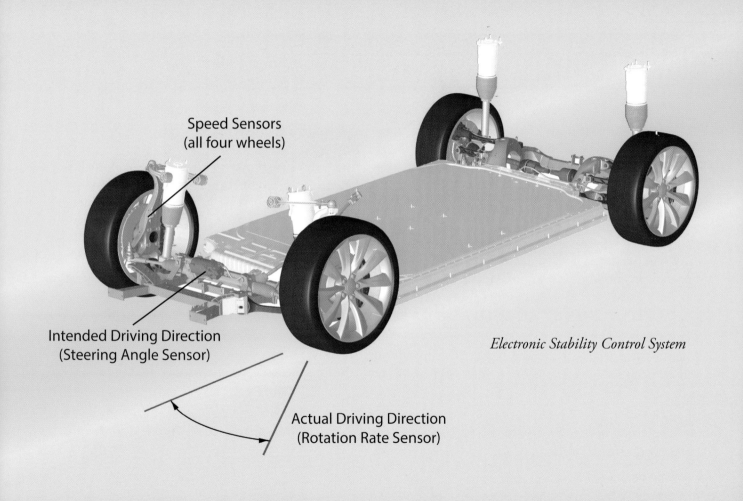

Speed Sensors
(all four wheels)

Intended Driving Direction
(Steering Angle Sensor)

Actual Driving Direction
(Rotation Rate Sensor)

*Electronic Stability Control System*

# Brakefest of Champions

Three separate braking systems provide the perfect combination of safety, great stopping power, control and comfort.

### Regenerative Braking

Most EVs and Hybrids offer a regenerative braking system. When braking is needed, the electric motor switches into generator mode. The resulting kinetic energy is converted into electricity to recharge the battery system and extend the range. Typically, this occurs when the brake pedal is partly depressed and the conventional brakes are applied when the pedal is pressed harder. This transition is very difficult to engineer and often results in poor brake feel.

Tesla engineers brilliantly combined the regenerative braking with the accelerator. Users can easily control

acceleration and deceleration only using the accelerator pedal. The transition between adding power and slowing down is quite seamless. Tesla also provides two levels of regeneration, but I recommend the standard level. It only takes a few minutes to feel comfortable and it helps maximize your range.

> **Cool Fact**
> The regenerative braking system automatically turns on the rear brake lights if the car decelerates quickly.

The Model S' superior regenerative braking system means that deceleration can be done mostly with the accelerator pedal. The more you lift your foot off the accelerator, the faster the car slows down.

Often the brake pedal is only needed when coming to a complete stop, such as going from about five mph to zero. Smoothly controlling your stops quickly becomes addictive. As a bonus, it puts almost no wear on the brakes. You can expect the brakes to last far longer than brakes on other vehicles.

When the battery has a maximum charge, regeneration is limited or disabled, since there is no place to store the extra energy. When this occurs, a yellow dashed line appears on the regeneration meter (green portion of the speedometer) to show when regeneration is limited. The yellow line disappears after a few miles of driving when full regeneration is available.

## Hydraulic Brakes

Similar to most other cars, the Models S includes a power assisted hydraulic brake system controlled by the left pedal. It includes an Anti-Lock Braking System, required of all cars today. Each wheel's large ventilated cast-iron rotors have four-piston fixed-calipers. These brakes deliver a fade-resistant 60 to zero mph distance of 108 feet (32 m), far shorter than most vehicles. It also does this magic with the right amount of pedal travel and feel.

## Parking Brake

The Model S includes an electronically actuated parking brake. This brake is engaged automatically when in Park, and disengaged automatically when in Drive mode. The system uses a single-piston sliding caliper brake on each rear wheel. This system is separate from other brakes and does not require power to remain engaged.

Parking Brake Caliper

Ventilated Rotor

Hydraulic Brake Caliper

*Rear Brake Components*

# Bumps in the Road

The Model S suspension systems offer that rare ability to provide both a great ride and taut handling. It starts with an almost perfect 48 percent front and 52 percent rear weight distribution. Tesla offers a choice of a standard spring/coil system, or an optional smart air suspension.

Smart air allows changing the ride height automatically to level the car under various loads and lowers the car as it accelerates. This improves the car's aerodynamics, which results in slightly increased range.

The air suspension can also be adjusted manually from the touch screen for low speeds. While not intended for off-road use, increased ride height allows you to negotiate an unusually bad road, poor transitions onto a steep driveway, or driving through thick snow. It's also useful if you have to traverse a lightly flooded road or park near unusually high front curbs. Once the speed exceeds 19 mph, the car automatically resumes its standard height.

The front suspension is a lightweight aluminum double-wishbone design. The rear uses an independent multi-link coil spring rear suspension. The combination delivers incredible handling while helping to absorb those nasty bumps in the road!

## Cool Fact

The Model S standard clearance of 6 inches exceeds many cars, and the air suspension allows it to go up to 7.3 inches of clearance, the territory of many SUVs!

*Front Air Suspension and Steering Linkage*

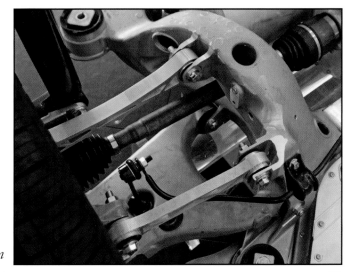

*Rear Air Suspension*

# Steer Me Right

Part of what makes a great car is the quality of the steering and road feedback. Often the desired "feel" varies wildly by owner, and can change based on road conditions. Some owners prefer an easy light touch for touring, while others want tight sports car handling with good road feedback.

Tesla managed to address a wide range of customer desires with multiple steering options. The Models S uses a variable ratio, speed sensitive, rack and pinion electronic power steering system. A driver can select the steering feel they want at any time – satisfying a wide range of users without compromise.

An electronic power steering system has a number of additional advantages over old hydraulic power steering systems. It uses about a tenth of the power, saves weight, and eliminates the need for a steering pump, high-pressure hoses and oil reservoir.

The steering wheel fully adjusts with power tilt and telescopic adjustments. With the Tech Package option, these settings are saved and restored for each user profile.

**Cool Fact**
Electronic steering systems are quiet and maintenance free.

*Electronic Steering Rack and Linkage*

# Heart of the Machine

The Model S is enthusiastically called a computer on wheels and the single best consumer gadget. The software and hardware are the core of the Model S experience. The car contains over fifty processors and embedded systems with software written in C code. It's the software that regulates the power flow between the motor and the battery pack. There's software for charge management, thermal management and other sophisticated controls. The end result is an incredible driving experience!

Another area of major advancement is the infotainment and instrumentation systems. The touchscreen display and instrument panel are built on NVIDIA's Tegra® processors running a modified Linux kernel with the Qt framework. The user interface offers intuitive Apple-like simplicity. These systems are completely independent from the vehicle dynamics software, adding further safety and reliability to the driving experience.

Over-the-air software upgrading is another welcome feature that distinguishes the Model S. Tesla regularly releases free updates that are loaded with new features that continue to make the car even better. Typically every two to three months, Tesla sends out a free update over the wireless connection. Last year's cars get the same new features as this year's cars. Navigation maps are always up to date. Refinements make a great experience even better!

## Hidden Secrets

Tap the Tesla logo to see the current software version and what's new in this release. On this same screen, press the model logo (60, 85, P85, P85+) for 15 seconds to open the Easter Egg!

*NVIDIA Visual Computing Module*
*with Quad-core Tegra® 3 processor*

# I'm Connected!

Many luxury vehicles offer a limited built-in cellular connection, but the Model S was the first to support full Internet connectivity on its huge 17-inch touch screen. The Model S was introduced with a 3G cellular connection and now supports WiFi connections. Tesla expects to offer faster data connectivity options in the future.

Downloading new features and software updates is a snap. Tesla also provides remote monitoring and vehicle diagnostic problem analysis. This allows the identification of problems and in some cases, remote fixes.

Owners enjoy free streaming music using Slacker or TuneIn. The song or artist is identified and its related album artwork appears. The connection allows viewing Google maps, real-time traffic status and satellite images. Even web browsing is supported.

For Signature car owners, Tesla offered a free year of data connectivity and three months of free data service for all other Model S owners. After the free trial period ends, Tesla offers a low-cost monthly data plan with unlimited data or owners can opt to use a WiFi tether to their personal cell phone.

### Legal Fact
In the USA, the web browser is not allowed to display streaming video to the driver.

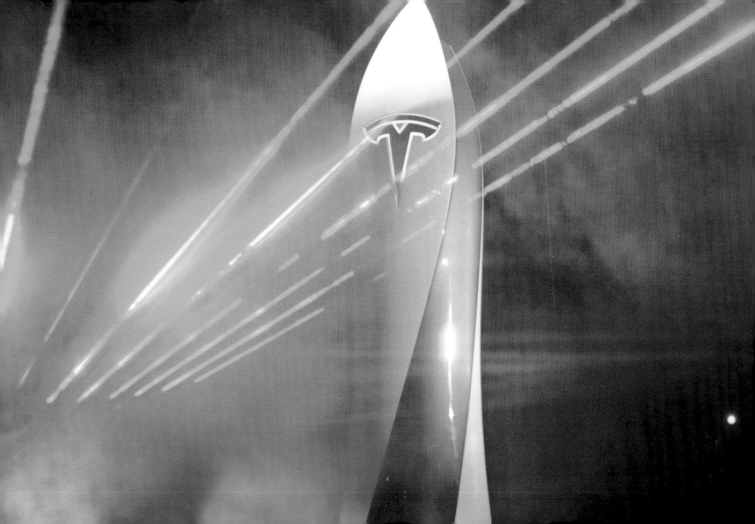

Fueling the Model S

# All Charged Up

Tesla carefully designed the Model S to make charging convenient whether at home or on the road. In the USA, every Model S comes with a mobile connector and two adapters for use in any home: a standard 120 volt home outlet adapter and a NEMA 14-50 240 volt outlet adapter. It's obviously preferable to charge using the faster 240 volt adapter. And for even faster charging, a Model S owner can get the optional High Power Wall Connector.

When away from home, Tesla supports multiple options: public charging stations, Tesla Supercharger stations and 90 second battery pack swapping at some Supercharger stations in the future. For public charging stations, every Model S includes a J1772 adapter, or you can purchase the optional CHAdeMO adapter.

A hidden charge port resides behind the left rear side taillight. The port is opened from within the car at the Touchscreen, or by simply depressing the button on the charging connector.

## Cool Fact

The connector is locked into place to prevent disconnection and theft of the cord while charging. Only when the FOB is nearby is the connector released.

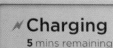

# Charging
**5** mins remaining

STOP CHARGING

↗ **39** mi/hr
+ **1** mi

230 mi

79 / 80 A
226 v

SET CHARGE LIMIT

SETTINGS FOR THIS LOCATION

### SCHEDULED CHARGING

OFF | ON

START CHARGING HERE A*

12:00 AM

### CHARGE CURRENT

▲
**80** A
▼

# Charging with the Mobile Connector

Every Model S comes with a Mobile Connector and multiple adapters. This allows charging at home or on the road. With a very long 18 foot (5.4 meter) cord, the mobile connector reaches most outlets in a garage or charging station. North American adapters allow charging from a 120 VAC outlet, a NEMA 14-50 240 VAC outlet or using a 240 VAC J1772 connector from public charging stations. Additional adapters for other types of 240 VAC outlets are available from Tesla. In Europe cars are equipped with adapters for IEC Blue single-phase and IEC Red 3-phase.

North American charging stations are mostly one of two variants, a Level 1, which is really just a 120 VAC outlet, and Level 2, a 240 VAC connection. Of the Level 2 stations, most, but not all in the USA, use the J1772 adapter. The Level 2 chargers are mostly

lower current 27 amp systems, but some support up to 80 amps. The car handles up to 40 amps with the standard single built-in charger. The optional twin charger handles up to 80 amps. Charging power is automatically lowered as the charge approaches 100% to extend battery life.

*North America: Best Charging Speed – Range per hour of charge*

| Power | With single or twin chargers | | | | | With twin chargers | | | |
|---|---|---|---|---|---|---|---|---|---|
| | 12 amps | 16 amps | 27 amps | 30 amps | 40 amps | 50 amps | 60 amps | 70 amps | 80 amps |
| 120 VAC | 5 miles | 6 miles | | | | | | | |
| | 7 km | 10 km | | | | | | | |
| 240 VAC | | | 21 miles | 23 miles | 31 miles | 39 miles | 47 miles | 54 miles | 62 miles |
| | | | 34 km | 37 km | 50 km | 63 km | 76 km | 87 km | 100 km |

*Europe: Best Charging Speed – Range per hour of charge*

| Power | 16 amps | 32 amps |
|---|---|---|
| IEC Blue, 230 V single phase | 19 km | 38 km |
| IEC Red, 400 V, 3-phase | 33 km | 67 km (Twin chargers required) |

*Mobile Connector Bundle with Adapters*

# Charging with the HPWC

Tesla offers an optional High-Power Wall Connector (HPWC) which doubles the speed of charging at home. It is directly wired to a home's electrical system and includes a fixed 20 foot (6 meter) connection cord and cord holder.

Normally, the HPWC is installed on a 230-240 VAC, 100 amp circuit, and draws up to 80 amps. Only cars equipped with the optional twin-chargers take advantage of this faster charge rate. For cars only equipped with the single charger, the HPWC still works, but is limited to 40 amps, similar to the mobile charger cable.

If a fault is detected, the indicator on the HPWC will light up red. In some cases, simply pressing the red reset button located on the bottom side may clear the fault.

At maximum power, the HPWC charges at the rate of 62 miles (100 km) per hour. For a Model S with an 85 kWh battery pack and twin chargers, the HPWC restores its EPA-certified 265 mile (426 km) range in roughly four to five hours.

## Cool Fact

For houses wired with limited power capacity, the HPWC is set to match the circuit breaker from 40 to 100 amps in ten amp increments.

TΞSLΛ

*High-Power Wall Connector*

# Wired Up

Ideally you'll want to charge up your Model S at home. While a 120 VAC outlet will function, the slow charging times make this impractical for most users. You'll want a 240 VAC connection, and the higher the amperage the better.

## Using an Existing Connection

Some garages may already be wired for a 240 VAC receptacle, perhaps for an electric dryer or welder. If the receptacle is located close enough to charge your car, no additional wiring may be necessary. Check your circuit breaker box to see the receptacle's amperage. Hopefully it's labeled and you can read the amperage from the circuit breaker. The chart on page 78 shows the charging time based on 240 VAC and the amperage. If this meets all your requirements, you may need to purchase a different adapter from Tesla to use your mobile connector.

## Wiring a New Connection

To wire a new receptacle or the Tesla HPWC, you'll need an electrician to run a wire from your breaker panel to the location that is convenient to charge your car. This location can be outdoors, in a carport or a garage. The receptacle/HPWC should be installed near the driver's side, rear of the car. For a 50 amp circuit, you would install a NEMA 14-50 receptacle.

Most users charge late at night, so unless the residence is inadequately wired, a 50 amp charging connection is usually not a problem for most residences built in the last 30 years. Older residences or going to the HPWC, which ideally uses a 100 amp circuit, could require an overall upgrade of the circuit and incoming power. Your electrician should advise you if the power is inadequate and if additional work is required.

## Tips and Considerations

- You'll need space in your circuit breaker box for two breakers (240 VAC requires two breakers).

- You may need to clear space to run the wires from the breaker box to the desired location (an electrician can advise the best routing).

- In most jurisdictions, you'll need a city permit for the electrical work. Don't let anyone talk you out of it as it helps ensure the work is done properly.

- If the receptacle is more than ten feet from the breaker panel, I recommend having the electrician install wiring one-size larger than required by code. The added cost is usually minimal. It will reduce the voltage drop to the receptacle for a slight increase in the charging speed and reduce the wire temperature.

- When installing the NEMA receptacle, tell the electrician to orient the grounding lug up.

- If installing a NEMA 14-50 now, but think you might install the HPWC sometime later, then go ahead and have the wires installed for a 100 amp circuit, and use a 50 amp breaker for now.

## Issues for Renters

Renters need to check with their landlord about adding a charging receptacle at your designated parking spot. Some landlords see the advantage of having this receptacle for future tenants, and may agree to let you have the work performed if you pay for it. Of course, this assumes you plan to stay long enough to make it worthwhile!

*One style of NEMA 14-50 receptacle in a metal box*

# Supercharging

The Model S has the longest range of any electric car on the road today. Superchargers extend the range even further. It's like a gas station with free gas! A Supercharger allows very fast charging by bypassing the internal charger and charging the battery with DC power.

Superchargers are found at popular locations such as shopping malls and rest stops along major routes. In September 2012, Tesla introduced its first Superchargers in six California locations. Tesla continues to expand its network both in United States and other countries where it sells vehicles such as Europe and Asia.

When introduced, Superchargers could charge a drained battery at the rate of 150 miles of range in 30 minutes. Within a year after its introduction, Supercharger stations were enhanced to charge 150 miles of range in 20 minutes, a 30% faster rate. JB Straubel, Tesla Chief Technology Officer, says this is not the last speed increase and expects charging speeds to continue to improve.

## User Tip

When selecting a Supercharger stall, pick a numbered stall where both A and B are both empty. For example, if stall 1A is occupied and 1B, 2A, and 2B are open, avoid stall 1B and choose 2A or 2B instead. The second car of a pair may only get 30 kW of power until the other car in the pair is nearly charged up.

Superchargers are also eco-friendly when a station gets its own solar charger canopy. Not surprising, the solar arrays come from SolarCity whose Chairman is Elon Musk. Tesla plans to make the system power neutral, so that each Supercharger station generates more energy than it needs.

Supercharging is free for life on all Model S equipped with 85 kWh battery pack and free for life after a one-time fee for 60 kWh models. Once again, Tesla is changing the car business model with its Supercharger network.

**"We are giving Model S the ability to drive almost anywhere for free on pure sunlight."**

*- Elon Musk*

# Charging with CHAdeMO

CHAdeMO is the name for a fast direct-current charging system. Ignoring the odd name, CHAdeMO offers the next fastest charging stations after the Tesla Superchargers. CHAdeMO is also referred to as Level 3 charging.

Developed in Japan, it's been deployed in Japan, parts of Europe and the Pacific Northwest of the United States. Nissan has also been rolling out public CHAdeMO chargers at select US dealerships. Originally intended to support the growing number of Leaf EVs, these dealer charging stations are available to anyone.

Tesla offers an optional CHAdeMO stand-alone adapter. It does not use the Mobile connector, as it fits between the large CHAdeMO connector and the car's charge port. Like Tesla's Superchargers, it does not use the on-board charger, but supplies power directly to the battery.

To use CHAdeMO, in addition to the Tesla adapter, the Model S must be Supercharger enabled. All models other than the S60 are Super-charger enabled, and the S60 can be enabled for a one-time fee. Similar to many public Level 1 and Level 2 chargers, you need to be registered on the charging network for the specific charger. Blink and ChargePoint are the primary networks in the USA.

The Model S gains about 150 miles of range per hour when charging at a CHAdeMO station.

## Cool Fact

CHAdeMO is an abbreviation of "CHArge de MOve", meaning Charge for Moving. It's also a pun in Japanese for "O cha demo ikaga desu ka". It translates to "How about some tea?" the time it takes to get 30 minutes of charge.

CHAdeMO

CHArJit

START    STOP

*CHAdeMO Ready to Charge*

# SuperSwapping

The Model S was designed from the beginning to be able to swap out the battery pack faster than filling up a gas tank. At the June 2013 news conference, Tesla demonstrated this capability. The Model S took about 90 seconds to make the battery swap, whereas an Audi A8 sedan took more than 4 minutes to refuel.

At select Supercharger stations, Tesla may offer a fully automated battery swap. It is expected to be priced around $70 - similar to the cost of 15 gallons of gas. The process involves swapping out a discharged battery with one that is fully charged.

Simply drive up, confirm the swap and 90 seconds later drive away. There is no need to leave the car during the entire brief process. When you return from a long trip, the swapping station returns your original battery, fully charged.

Tesla plans to provide the option of keeping the loaner battery for an additional fee, less the trade-in value of the old battery based on age and usage. At the news conference, Elon Musk reiterated Tesla's policy that battery pack swapping would be supported on all past and future Tesla Model S cars. Tesla believes it's essential that customers have the same sense of freedom without range anxiety as they do with a gasoline car. This is the reason for Tesla's long distance travel options: free Supercharging or low-cost SuperSwapping. Tesla once again is leading the way with multiple electric fueling options.

## Cool Fact

A swapping station could hold up to 50 battery packs at a time and costs around $500,000 to build.

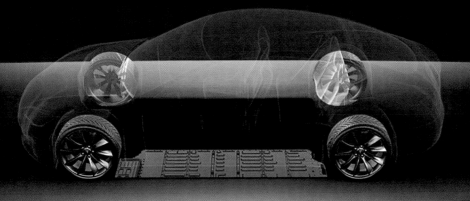

INSTALLING BATTERY

# On the Range

Range anxiety is one of the most common reasons why someone is unwilling to buy an EV. While this is often a valid concern for non-Tesla EVs because of their limited range, this misconception needs correcting for those buying a Model S. Tesla does more to solve this concern than any other EV maker.

A study used by GM when designing the Chevy Volt determined that 78% of American commuters drove 40 miles or less per day. The US Census Bureau defined a "megacommuter" as someone who drove at least 100 miles round trip per day. Based on the 2006-2010 census data, only one in 122 full-time workers have such a commute. So a Model S easily handles a driver's daily needs but this is a legitimate concern with other short range EVs.

The EPA range for the S85 is 265 miles per charge – a mix of highway and city driving that includes speeds up to 80 mph and use of the AC and heater. Your mileage may vary! You get more range if you use cruise control than if you drive at inconsistent speeds. If driving in freezing or extreme heat, the HVAC system may reduce the range by 10%. In mountain driving, expect about eight miles of range loss per 1000 feet of elevation climb, but you'll get most of this back on the way down due to regenerative braking.

**Cool Fact**

Use of the radio and lights on the Model S have negligible effect on range. So no worries, keep enjoying your music!

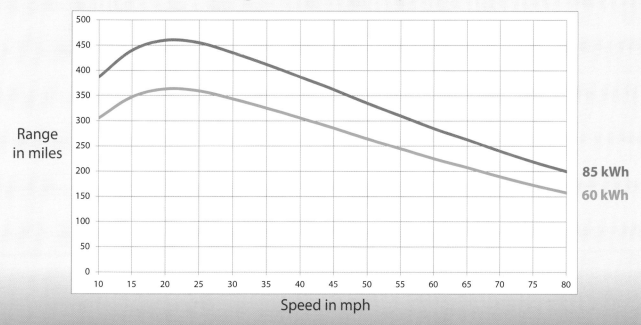

# Range vs. Constant Speed

**Range in miles** (y-axis)

**Speed in mph** (x-axis)

85 kWh
60 kWh

**Conditions**
- Constant speed (such as using cruise control)
- Flat ground, no wind
- Climate control off or using vent only (no heat or ac)
- 300 lbs of vehicle load (driver plus passenger or cargo)
- Windows up, sunroof closed
- Tires inflated to recommended pressures
- New battery pack (<1 year, <25,000 miles)
- 60 kWh estimated from 85 kWh

A fully charged 85-kWh Model S gets 300 miles of range on flat ground going 55 mph. If you drive slowly, Model S owners have been able to exceed 400 miles on a charge! Ok, no one wants to drive slowly, but the Model S really does let us drive without compromise.

For most people, the Model S offers plenty of range to go to work, lunch, errands, return home, and make another trip at night – all on a single charge. Most Model S owners never bother charging anywhere other than at home.

If you need to charge away from home, the Model S built in charger works with 240 VAC connections and thousands of charging stations throughout the USA such as the Chargepoint and Blink charging networks. In reality, these are rarely needed or used by Model S owners. The charger also works with a standard 120 VAC outlet, although the charging rate is quite slow.

For longer trips, Tesla's Superchargers are strategically located to provide a fast charge, just like a gas station. Superchargers provide 150 miles of range in about twenty to thirty minutes. If that's not fast enough, Tesla demonstrated a battery swapping system that swaps in a fully charged battery in about 90 seconds! All Model S cars are already designed to work with automated SuperSwappers.

The true source of range anxiety comes from a lack of a Supercharger on every street corner. We are used to seeing gas stations available everywhere. There are far more charging stations besides Tesla's Superchargers than people realize. There are currently over 50,000 non-residential slow charging points and over 2000 fast chargers around the world. People forget that when Ford introduced the Model A in 1903 there were no gas stations either. But that didn't stop people from buying his cars. Tesla is busy rolling out a national network of charging stations in each country of operation.

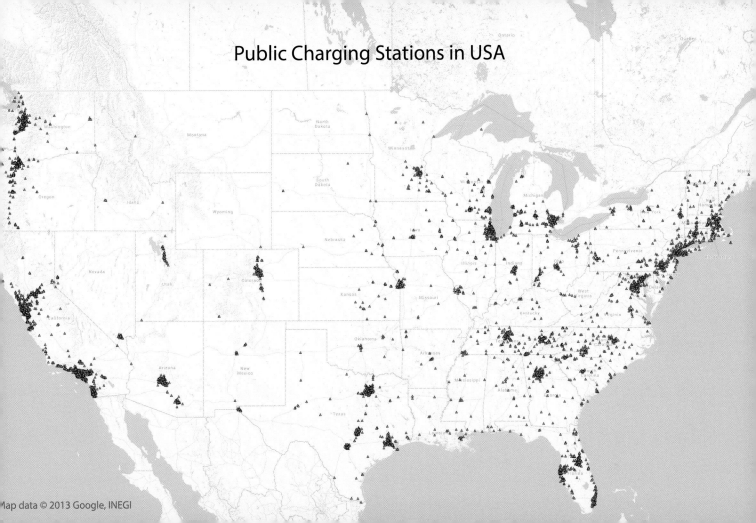

Public Charging Stations in USA

Map data © 2013 Google, INEGI

Getting the Model S

# Myth Busters

Although electric vehicles have been around for over 100 years, the current generation is new to most people. Here are a few misconceptions we'll try to correct!

## Myth: EVs are slow

Different cars (both EVs and ICE) can be high-performance or slow dogs. In the case of the Model S, it's one of the fastest cars you can buy for the money and usually outperforms other competitive sport sedans and yet still provides the equivalent of 89 mpg.

**BUSTED!**

## Myth: Short Battery Life

Will my battery pack last as long as I own the car? The Model S battery pack was specifically designed for longevity. Tesla uses a liquid cooling system to increase the life of its battery pack. Keeping lithium batteries in a full state of charge and hot may reduce the life of a battery, but these extremes are rare with the huge Tesla battery pack. Tesla's software prevents damage from overcharging or running the battery too low. Tesla also backs up their battery with a eight year "no fault" warranty except for deliberate misuse.

**BUSTED!**

## Myth: Lithium-Ion batteries self ignite

A handful of lithium-ion battery fires in laptops occurred about 10 years ago, caused by a manufacturing defect on a tiny percentage of batteries. More recent concerns have come from the Boeing 787 Dreamliner battery design. Lithium batteries have considerable energy storage, and should a fully charged cell internally fail due to a short, it can rapidly discharge, heat up, and could even catch fire.

Tesla pioneered the way to make a lithium battery pack safe even if a cell were to fail. This involves having a pack architecture based on many small cells with multiple layers of safety and protection. First, Tesla uses higher quality automotive grade cells over those used in common products like laptops. The Model S uses more than 7000 lower energy cells instead of a few large high-energy cells used in other less safe designs. It's easier to maintain an even temperature in a small cell reducing the possibility of a thermal runaway situation. Each individual cell in the Model S is fused. Each cell is also physically separated with gaps and thermal insulation. Even if one cell fails, it does not affect adjacent cells. The battery pack is also liquid cooled, so if a cell starts to fail, the cooling system helps keep it from overheating. Lastly, the entire battery pack is sealed in a strong steel/aluminum structure.

In over 100 million road miles and over 140 million cells in use with the Model S, I am unaware of a single instance of a cell self-igniting.

**BUSTED!**

## Myth: The Model S is likely to catch fire

Every vehicle in production must store fuel on board to power the vehicle. In the case of ICE vehicles, this is typically gasoline, diesel, or in some cases, compressed natural gas. These fuels are very flammable and any breach of the fuel tank or fuel lines usually causes a fire that destroys the vehicle and often harms the occupants.

Lithium batteries store the electrical energy 'fuel' for the Model S. The total amount of energy is about a tenth of that stored in a typical gasoline tank. That's because an EV is far more efficient at converting electrical energy into motion. In an ICE car, most of the fuel energy is lost to heat, noise and the chemical reactions that create pollution. In the end some of that energy is actually converted to motion.

Raw Lithium is quite combustible and burns when exposed to air. About one percent of the battery is made from lithium, but it is in a form that is not all that combustible and is not a concern. On the other hand, electrolyte is quite flammable, and should the cell's metal casing be breached, it may catch fire. A single cell contains very little electrolyte. Should a group of cells be breached at the same time, due to a major crash, it is possible for the electrolyte to fuel a fire.

Now onto the real world! In the first 100 million road miles with the Model S, there have been only two fires. One occurred when a car on the freeway drove over a large metal object that pierced a three inch hole in the car's quarter inch thick bottom plate. The driver was able to come to a stop, exit the vehicle and was unharmed. A portion of the battery pack caught fire due to major physical damage to the battery pack. The fire did not enter the cabin. A second event occurred in Mexico when a driver crashed though a cement wall and into a tree totaling the car. The driver exited the car unharmed.

Using the latest data available in the USA, there are reports of 187,500 vehicles a year catching fire on the highway in 2011 according to the National Fire Protection Association. Many more go unreported or occur off the highway. The US Department of Transportation reports that Americans drove 2.9 trillion miles a year in 2011.

Using these numbers, 6.5 ICE vehicle fires occur for every 100 million miles of travel. Comparing this with the Model S of two fires for 100 million miles of travel means ICE vehicles catch fire more than three times as often as the Model S.

**Myth: Refueling takes a long time**

With SuperSwappers, a battery swap takes less time than a gasoline fill up. Ok, SuperSwappers are not really deployed yet, but Superchargers are available in a number of locations for long trips. Fueling take slightly longer – 20 to 30 minutes for 150 miles of range. What is lost in this debate is that 99 percent of the time your Model S is charged at home. You will rarely use any other charging, except for long trips. This means every day you leave with a full 'tank'! No need to ever visit the gas station again!

## Myth: EVs are not Green

Some claim that more $CO_2$ is produced than similar ICE vehicles due to EV manufacturing and recharging.

A number of studies conclude that even in states with the dirtiest electric grids, driving a Model S produces less $CO_2$ than similar ICE cars. Many states and other countries generate electricity in a much cleaner way due to solar, wind, hydro and other means. Many homes are also solar powered, reducing emissions to zero for those users.

While some $CO_2$ is produced during the production of any vehicle, Tesla manufactures its car in California, where the electrical power is dramatically cleaner than most other car producing states.

Not only are EVs pollution free, they produce less $CO_2$ in production and over the entire life of the car. Our section Clean and Green on page 106 explains this in more depth.

**BUSTED!**

## Myth: I'll be stranded

Often called range anxiety, it occurs when you think you will run out of energy on a trip. This is true of any vehicle ICE or EV. The Model S EPA range of 206 or 265 miles depending on the model, is sufficient for most user's needs.

To avoid getting stranded, the Model S warns the user well before you run out of power, just like a low-fuel warning light on many ICE cars. The Model S shows you how many miles are available before empty. Even when you get to zero miles, the Model S delivers another 10-15 miles of emergency reserve power.

Unlike an ICE car that is dependent on finding a gas station when low on fuel, the Model S can plug into any of the millions of 120 or 240 volt outlets, thousands of public charging stations, or a superchargers to get more fuel.

**BUSTED!**

## Myth: Hacking could disable or steal a car

Yes, it may be possible, but this is true of all cars today. Every car produced uses computers to control the security system, propulsion and many other systems. The fact that every car is somewhat different reduces the chance that even if some hack were devised, it would only affect a small part of the automotive ecosystem. You'd need a target car to reverse engineer and figure out the hack – an expensive proposition to start with. For more on this interesting topic, check out *autosec.org*.

If you want to steal a car, drag it onto a flatbed and take it away to the chop shop. There is no need to go to the trouble of attempting a technically complex hack.

## Myth: I'll be stuck in the apocalypse

During a power failure, everyone is in the same boat. You'll be left with what gasoline or electrical power is left in your vehicle. Gas stations are not too useful, since the pumps will be dead. Even if you can find gas, it may be contaminated or quickly consumed by others. For EVs, houses with solar electricity could provide a charge during the daytime. If you can get to a solar powered Supercharger, you'll be king of the road!

Now for comfort, the Model S is unbeatable. If the outage is only for a short time, you can relax, listen to music, access the Web, and even sleep in the car at the perfect temperature. Since EVs do not produce carbon monoxide, it's safe to keep the climate control running in a garage.

# Reasons Not to Buy

The Tesla Model S is not for everyone. Here are some of the reasons why it may not be the right car for you.

- You are the owner of a gas station and get gas for free.

- You are a mechanic and enjoy spending lots of time and money fixing your car.

- You are a parent with toddlers and you're happy you can't hear them screaming over the loud engine noise of your car.

- You are an oil executive and it would look bad to be environmentally responsible to your shareholders.

- You are sensitive to sunlight and want to contribute your fair share of smog to keep the brown haze over the city.

- You are a sheik in some oil-rich country, so you want to encourage gasoline usage to drive up prices.

- As a grateful politician who receives campaign contributions from the Automobile Dealers Association, you need to vote against anything that is consumer friendly relating to buying a car.

- You are in the fossil fuel extraction business and you really don't care about the occasional environmental catastrophe, so long as insurance covers it.

*Deepwater Horizon Oil Platform Fire*

# Alternatives

When it comes to luxury sports sedan, the Model S easily beats out the competition! It beat a BMW M5 in a drag race. The EPA rated the 2013 Model S 60 as having the highest fuel economy in the large car category. And it's the only sports sedan that holds five adults and two children.

In its first full year of production, the Model S outperformed all pure electric cars with its range and fast-charging batteries. One of the non-Tesla EVs with the longest range is the Toyota RAV4 with about half the range of the Model S. In the 2013 Canada to Mexico electric car race, the Model S crushed its competition which included a Zero S electric motorcycle, Toyota RAV4 EV, Mitsubishi i-MiEV and two Nissan Leafs.

There are alternatives depending on what you're willing to give up:

- A luxury hybrid car with both an electric motor and gas engine may offer some competition. But hybrids still use gasoline and create pollution. Hybrids are also far more complex than EVs or stand-alone ICE cars and may have higher maintenance costs.

- Compact electric cars and plug-in hybrids have limited electric range and usually sacrifice luxury, space, comfort, features and style.

- Gasoline luxury sports cars start to approach the performance of the Model S, but at the expense of fuel economy and the environment.

Because the Tesla Model S created a new category of car, the electric luxury sport sedan, it's quite hard to find a true competitor.

# USA Competitive Vehicle Analysis

| Sport Sedan | Net Cost[1] | 0-60 MPH | Cargo Cu. Ft.[2] | Range in miles | EPA MPG Combined | Fuel Cost[3], 12,000 Miles | Annualized cost[4], 8-years |
|---|---|---|---|---|---|---|---|
| Tesla S60 | $63,570 | 5.9 | 31.6 | 208 | 95 | $453 | $6,015 |
| Tesla S85 | $73,570 | 5.4 | 31.6 | 265 | 89 | $467 | $6,905 |
| Tesla P85 | $83,570 | 4.2 | 31.6 | 265 | 89 | $467 | $7,780 |
| | | | | | | | |
| BMW M5* | $92,425 | 4.3 | 14.0 | 337 | 16 | $2,783 | $10,870 |
| Cadillac CTS-V Premium* | $69,995 | 5.1 | 13.7 | 391 | 21 | $2,162 | $8,286 |
| Mercedes E63 AMG* | $90,705 | 4.2 | 15.9 | 401 | 19 | $2,344 | $10,820 |
| Porsche Panamara S | $94,175 | 4.9 | 11.9 | 401 | 19 | $2,344 | $10,584 |
| Audi S7* | $81,095 | 4.5 | 24.5 | 396 | 20 | $2,227 | $9,322 |

[1] Net Cost for 2013 (*2014) base vehicles, plus destination, gas guzzler tax, rebates, but with NO options. Federal EV rebate of $7500 included. Does not include repairs and maintenance, smog tests if any, interest on loan if any, local taxes, or local rebates for EVs (0-$7,500).

[2] Cargo space with the seats in the upright position. With the seats down, cargo space on the Model S expands to a total of 63.4 cubic feet.

[3] Annual premium gas costs based on $3.711/gallon from AAA national average October 18, 2013; Electricity for 75% of mileage, rest free at Superchargers. Electric rates vary by location, using $0.118 national average in 2011, and could be far less with off-peak charging in some locations or by using solar.

[4] Assumes a 30% resale value at the end of 8-years with 96,000 miles.

# Clean and Green

Overwhelming scientific data indicates global warming is real and is caused primarily by humans. So concludes former climate skeptic, Dr. Richard Muller, UC Berkeley physics professor. The fossil fuel and related industry lobbyists have copied the tobacco lobby tactics to confuse the general public with counter claims and dubious studies. This is reminiscent of how we were told tobacco wasn't harmful to people. The public is catching on. As the saying goes, if it looks like a duck and walks like a duck, it's a duck.

To be fair, there is quite a bit of disagreement on what can be done, how it should be done, and what social and environmental impacts are appropriate.

Carbon Dioxide, $CO_2$, contributes about 25% of the greenhouse effects. In the atmosphere, $CO_2$ has increased by about 37% in the last 180 years, with most of that in the last 40 years. China and India are the 1st and 4th largest producers of $CO_2$ gases. The United States is in 2nd place with the European Union in 3rd place. These four contribute 62% of annual $CO_2$ emissions!

Road transport is responsible for about 17% of $CO_2$ emissions. In the USA, automobiles are the second largest source of $CO_2$ pollution each year. What's more frightening is to imagine how much more $CO_2$ would be produced if all the potential Indian and Chinese people start driving gas cars too! Adoption of electric cars is an important component in reducing $CO_2$ emissions.

A few vocal critics claim that carbon emitted from obtaining and converting fossil fuel into electricity to recharge EV batteries exceeds the reduction in $CO_2$ obtained from driving an EV. Numerous scientific studies have shown this to be not true in USA. Crunching the numbers I came to the same conclusion.

## $CO_2$ production by ICE vehicles and the Model S

A gallon of gasoline creates 19.6 pounds of $CO_2$ from burning and another 2.5 pounds in refining. There's additional $CO_2$ produced from extraction, pre and post refinery transport and pumping, but we'll ignore those portions since I couldn't find a reliable source for those values. So a gallon of gas makes at least 19.6 plus 2.5, or 22.1 lbs of $CO_2$. Diesel engines produce about 14% more $CO_2$ per gallon of fuel than gasoline engines. These emissions are unrelated to EPA environmental controls, so the same results occur for any fuel burning vehicle of any age.

| Vehicle (Automatic Transmission) | EPA MPG | $CO_2$ lb/mile | Annual lbs $CO_2$ |
|---|---|---|---|
| Cadillac CTS-V | 16 | 1.381 | 16,600 |
| BMW M5 | 16 | 1.381 | 16,600 |
| Mercedes-Benz E63 AMG | 19 | 1.163 | 14,000 |
| Audi A8 | 21 | 1.052 | 12,700 |
| Infiniti Q50 | 23 | 0.961 | 11,500 |

All vehicles 2014 Model Year, EPA MPG combined

Our analysis of $CO_2$ emissions from gas cars uses the combined EPA MPG values, although most users get worse results. The results in the table are based on vehicles with automatic transmissions. The annual numbers are based on 12,000 miles of driving.

Electrical generation with coal produces the most $CO_2$ while solar, hydroelectric, nuclear, and wind power produce no $CO_2$. Different states in the US produce electricity with different mixes. Vermont produces the least $CO_2$ per MW-h and North Dakota the most.

| Tesla Vehicles | EPA kWh/mi | Annual lbs of $CO_2$ from Charging | | |
|---|---|---|---|---|
| | | Vermont | California | North Dakota |
| Model S60 | 0.35 | 10 | 2,500 | 9,200 |
| Model S85 | 0.38 | 11 | 2,700 | 10,100 |

Values include a 7% electrical distribution and transmission loss.

Comparing the two tables of vehicle $CO_2$ production, it's clear that the Model S produces a fraction of the $CO_2$ that a similar luxury ICE vehicle does in most parts of the country. There is a great deal of work being done to reduce $CO_2$ emissions at power plants and increase renewable energy sources. $CO_2$ from charging will go down significantly over the next five to ten years.

Of course, if you charge a Model S from a home's solar system or at a solar powered Supercharger station, then there is no $CO_2$ produced whatsoever!

**Hot Air**
Washington D.C. ranks as the highest in $CO_2$ emissions for electrical generation even exceeding North Dakota!

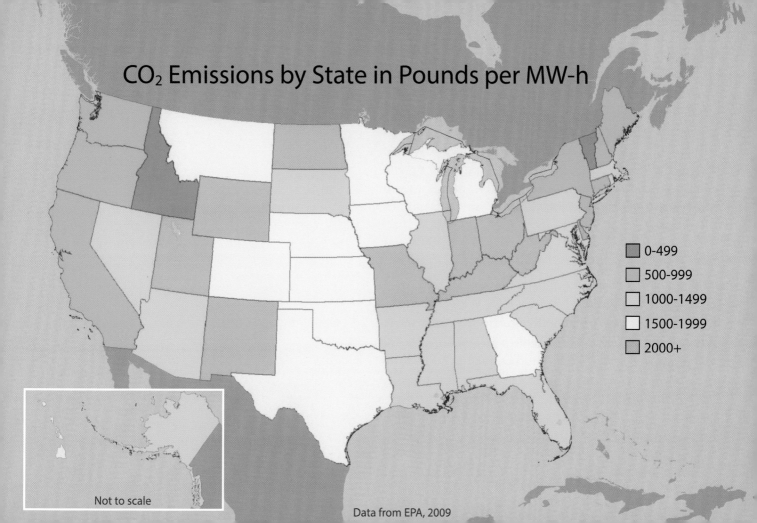

# CO$_2$ Emissions by State in Pounds per MW-h

0-499
500-999
1000-1499
1500-1999
2000+

Not to scale

Data from EPA, 2009

## CO₂ From Manufacturing

The manufacturing of aluminum for a vehicle produces 1200 lbs more $CO_2$ than a similar sized steel vehicle. Using aluminum improves fuel economy, which also reduces $CO_2$. The net result is that aluminum vehicles reduce the lifetime amount of $CO_2$ produced. Because aluminum is more expensive than steel, it is only used in luxury cars such as the Model S, BMW M5 and Audi A8.

Another argument made against EVs is that the manufacture of the materials specific to an EV, such as its lithium batteries, creates more $CO_2$ than the vehicle saves when driven over its lifetime. Likewise $CO_2$ is created during the manufacture of the complicated ICE car with its hundreds of engine and transmission parts, and special oils and fluids. A few conflicting studies attempt to quantify the carbon cost to manufacture an EV versus a gas car but to date there is no clear scientific consensus. What's needed is a rigorous scientific study based on the actual components used in a Tesla Model S against all parts in a ICE vehicle.

A significant reduction in carbon emissions can clearly be achieved through a combination of worldwide adoption of pure electric cars like the Model S coupled with cleaner power plant generation such as solar or natural gas based power plants.

### Hot Fact
A gallon of gas weights about 6.25 lbs. When gas burns, it chemically combines with oxygen from the air to produce 19.6 lbs of $CO_2$ and 8 lbs of water vapor, along with other pollutants.

# Award Show

We're not sure any other car has garnished so many awards so quickly! Here's a sampling of the honors bestowed on the Model S.

- Automobile Magazine's 2013 Car of the Year

- 2013 World Green Car of the Year

- Time Magazine Best Inventions of the Year 2012

- Yahoo! Autos 2013 Car of the Year

- CNET Tech Car of the Year for 2012

- Green Car Reports' Best Car To Buy 2013

- Popular Science's Auto Grand Award Winner - Best of What's New list 2012.

- Motor Trend 2013 Car of the Year

- 2013 AutoGuide.com Reader's Choice overall Car of the Year

- 2013 AutoGuide.com Reader's Choice categories of Luxury Car of the Year and Green Car of the Year

- Consumer Reports 2013 Top-rated car

- Natural Resources Canada 2013 EcoENERGY for Vehicles Awards in the full-size category

## Cool Fact
Motor Trend's Car of the Year award was the first given to a non-ICE car in 64 years!

10BEST CARS FOR 2013
CAR AND DRIVER
JANUARY 2013
SUMMER WINES
PAGE 8
TESLA MODEL S TOP-RATED CAR
Page 56
Automobile
Automobile of the Year
2013 Automobile
THE ELECTRIFYING
Tesla Model S
AS QUICK AS AN M5 . AS SMOOTH AS A LEXUS . NO GAS

# Media Admiration

"There's no other way to put it: Tesla's Model S luxury Sedan is spectacular."

*Chris Woodyard – USA Today*

"Actually, the Model S can blow away almost anything."

*David Zenlea – Automobile Magazine*

"By any measure, the Tesla Model S is a truly remarkable automobile, perhaps the most accomplished all-new luxury car since the original Lexus LS 400."

*Angus MacKenzie – Motor Trend*

"Tesla Model S, a car that shows superb technology throughout while also challenging our conceptions of how a car should work."

*Wayne Cunningham, Antuan Goodwin and Brian Cooley - CNET*

"We could never tire of punching the accelerator and having the car instantly pick up speed."

*Nauman Farooq – AutoGuide.com*

"Its pinpoint handling is reminiscent of a Porsche. The beautifully crafted interior calls to mind that of an Audi. And it's the quietest car we've tested since the Lexus LS."

*Consumer Reports*

"Beautiful, well-crafted, cool, and seriously fast, the Model S isn't just the most important car of the year. It's the most important car America has made in an entire lifetime."

*Jason Cammisa - Road & Track*

# Unusual Reasons to Buy

Here are a few ideas that may sway you to buy a Model S.

- Lose weight by avoiding the mini-mart twice a week when you no longer have to fill up your ICE car.

- Long trips are more enjoyable when the fuel is free via Superchargers.

- When depressed at least you can't die from carbon monoxide poisoning in your garage when running the Model S. Of course, it's hard to be depressed when you own a Model S!

- Supporting oil producing regimes is just not your thing.

- Help lower the price of gas for friends and neighbors by using less of it.

- You love that there's no annoying "I Agree" legalize screen every time you start the car.

- You'd like to carry a large item like a 65" flat screen TV, water heater or twin bed, but don't want to strap it to the top of the car. They all fit easily in the Model S, but maybe not all at once!

- You love that the Model S continuously gets new features without having to buy a new car every year.

- You prefer to avoid the hassle and expense of oil and filter changes every 5000 miles.

- You like the absence of paw prints on the hood from cats seeking a warm place to sleep.

- The thrill of instant get-up-and-go is intoxicating.

# Pick Your Flavor

Tesla produces four editions of the Model S:

**Models S P85/P85+** are the performance editions offering the highest speed and acceleration The Performance Plus package option further enhances the handling and adds a few miles of range.

| Specification | P85+ | P85 | S85 | S60 |
|---|---|---|---|---|
| Energy Storage | 85 kWh | 85 kWh | 85 kWh | 60 kWh |
| 0-60 mph time | 4.2 sec | 4.2 sec | 5.4 sec | 5.9 sec |
| Top Speed | 130 mph | 130 mph | 125 mph | 120 mph |
| EPA Range in miles | 271-277* | 265 | 265 | 208 |
| Supercharging | Included | Included | Included | Optional |
| High Performance drive inverter | Included | Included | n/a | n/a |
| Battery Warranty, 8 years or miles | unlimited miles | unlimited miles | unlimited miles | 125,000 miles |

\* EPA rating is 265 miles; Tesla states it gets an additional 6-12 miles due to tires.

**Model S 85** includes the same 85 kWh battery as the P85/P85+, but offers a little less acceleration and a slightly lower maximum speed.

**Model S 60** is the lowest cost edition and offers about 22 percent less range. While still having impressive acceleration, maximum speed and acceleration are lower than other models. To keep the price lower, Supercharging is an optional item.

### Cool Fact

Originally a 40 kWh edition was planned, but due to low demand, it was dropped. Customers who ordered the 40 kWh were given a car with a 60 kWh battery that was software limited to act like 40 kWh, with an option to upgrade to 60 kWh.

# Build it Your Way

Tesla, like any car manufacturer, offers quite a few options. Unlike other manufacturers, the Models S is built to order, so you select only the options you want! We'll leave the colors and style choices for you to ponder, but we'll examine other available options in North America. Options differ slightly in Europe and Asia.

| Option | Pros | Cons |
|---|---|---|
| S85 or S60 model | S85 delivers more power; more range; higher maximum speed; unlimited miles warranty on battery; and includes Supercharging; S60 is lower in cost and is slightly more efficient | S60 range may not be enough for your needs |

| Option | Pros | Cons |
|---|---|---|
| Performance 85 | Even more power; Higher maximum speed; | Costs even more than the S60 or S85 models. |
| Performance 85+ | When you want the ultimate in sport handling | Requires tech package, air suspension, and 21" tires (see below) |
| 21" Wheels over 19" | Looks really cool; Increased traction and improved handling | Easy to damage; Short tread life; Ride may be slightly harsher |
| 19" Primacy Tire Upgrade | These low rolling resistance tires boost range by another 3 percent (8 miles for S85/P85) | Extra cost on S60 model |

| Option | Pros | Cons |
| --- | --- | --- |
| Panoramic Roof | Ultra wide opening; blocks 98% of visible light when closed; Increased headroom | Slightly noisier |
| Subzero Weather Package | Recommended if you drive often in freezing weather or would like rear seat heaters | |
| Premium Interior Lighting | Cool look with ambient lighting | |
| Leather over Cloth Seats | Smoother, luxurious feel; Should last longer; Easier to slide in and out | Not cow friendly; Sticky in high-heat & humidity |
| Performance Seats | Upgrade to leather seats adds contrasting piping and Alcantara on the seat's side bolsters | Leather side bolsters make it easier to slide into the seat |

| Option | Pros | Cons |
| --- | --- | --- |
| Extended Leather Trim | Adds Nappa leather to dash, driver airbag cover and armrests; ups the luxury value | Not cow friendly; Dashboard leather may not hold up as well over time (sun damage) |
| Alcantara Headliner | Replaces standard fabric (which is still quite nice) with upgraded synthetic suede (even nicer) | |
| Wood or Carbon Fiber Décor | A nice visual upgrade; Piano black default shows fingerprints | |
| Tech Package | Many features including navigation, Homelink, seat position memory, power folding mirrors, power liftgate, etc. | Extra cost but many have regretted not getting this option. |
| Fog Lights | Recommended if you live in foggy weather | |

| Option | Pros | Cons |
|--------|------|------|
| Parking Sensors | Warns if you get too close to the front or rear bumpers. | |
| Ultra High Fidelity Sound | Higher quality sound; More power and speakers; XM Radio | |
| Smart Air Suspension | Adjust height to avoid bad transitions and handle dirt roads; Automatic load leveling; May increase range slightly | May be costly if repair needed after warranty ends |
| Rear Facing Seats | Carry 5 adults and 2 children; Folds into trunk well when not needed | Consumes a small amount of luggage space |
| Drop-in Center Console | Adds place to store more stuff; additional cup holders | Open area may be handy for bags and purses |

| Option | Pros | Cons |
|--------|------|------|
| Yacht Floor | Replaces the center carpet with a décor matching plate adding a bit of extra style | Can't be seen if using a center console |
| Carbon Fiber Spoiler (P85/P85+ only) | Adds additional rear traction and stability at high speeds; makes P85 more distinctive | Tiny range reduction of about 0.4 percent |
| Paint Armor | Protective film helps reduce paint damage | Seams may be visible, especially on colors like white |
| Twin Chargers with HPWC | Allows home charging at twice the rate of single charger | Requires HPWC installation and 100 amp circuit for full benefit |
| Super-charging option on S60 | Allows long trips with free fuel | Unneeded if only traveling around town |

# First Drive

Even if you've read all the great things I have to say about the Model S, you'll still need to take a drive to see if it really is the right car for you. You'll need to visit one of Tesla's showrooms to get a test drive, or have an owner-friend provide a drive!

Now for the test drive. You'll first notice there is no key or start button. The FOB is automatically detected as you approach the car, and when you sit in the driver's seat and press the brake pedal, the car turns on.

On the drive lever, you select Drive, Neutral, Reverse or press in for Park. The parking brake is automatically engaged in park and disengaged when you drive. There is no manual hand brake to bother with.

Be sure to adjust the seat and mirrors before taking off. Tray tables should be in an upright position. When you're out on the road and it's safe to do so, stomp on the accelerator for a total blast of smooth power. This never gets old!

Pay attention to the silky smooth transition from acceleration to regeneration by simply applying less pressure on the accelerator. Most drivers love how it feels after a fairly short time. Notice how quiet it is. Even if you currently own a high-end luxury car, the Tesla is even quieter. The sporty handling is solid with little body roll. Adjust the steering feel to your personal desire. The only bad part is how much you'll want to buy it afterwards!

***Cool Fact***
Tesla states that 25% of the users who test drive the car, buy one.

# The Upgradeable Car

Until Tesla came along, automakers made you buy a new car to get new or improved features. Tesla, on the other hand, designed their cars to be upgradeable from the start. Tesla recognized that today's modern cars are run mostly by software. So they designed a remote software update capability into the Model S. Batteries are the biggest cost in an EV. So Tesla also designed the battery pack to be upgradeable. The Model S may never become obsolete!

**Software** - Except for Tesla, car manufacturers, rarely update software, and often only to fix serious bugs. Tesla's fresh approach allows updating every car produced to the latest software. This means as new software features are created, every car gets upgraded with the latest features! You don't even need to visit a service center because updates are provided over-the-air via the built in cellular connection or WiFi. For example, in the spring of 2013, Tesla created an app for monitoring the car from a cellphone.

Of course new car buyers get this added feature, but so do all existing Model S owners. The software support was downloaded automatically to every Model S sold.

**The Battery** - JB Straubel, Tesla's CTO, noted that batteries improved by roughly 40% in four years between the launch of the Roadster and Model S. In anticipation of future battery improvements, Tesla designed the car to offer the possibility of upgrades to all Model S owners. With the SuperSwapper battery swapping system, for a fee, an owner may be able to quickly replace the battery pack with one that offers more range or quicker charging.

### Cool Fact
The battery is non-toxic and landfill safe. It is sold to recyclers at the end of its long life to recover useful elements.

# Making it Right

With a new car company and car, reliability is a concern, but not with Tesla. Tesla designed the Model S like it's going into space where failure is not an option! It's not surprising since Tesla's CEO, Elon Musk also runs SpaceX. Tesla's design philosophy is to exceed automobile engineering standards.

The Model S uses high quality parts and materials expected in a luxury car. The car also uses far fewer mechanical parts and that greatly boosts long-term reliability too. For example, the Tesla motor has one moving part, the rotor. A typical modern V8 engine has over 130 moving parts, many of which are always under high-stress. Add in more high-wear parts like the transmission and exhaust systems, and it's no wonder ICE cars need so much servicing!

People forget but early Japanese cars had a reputation for breaking down. It took Toyota over five years to reverse that image in USA. In contrast, Tesla maintains a stellar reputation for quality and reliability on every car it's brought to market as attested to by car and customer reviews. If customers encounter any problem on the Model S, Tesla quickly corrects those issues at their service centers or by sending out Tesla rangers to the customer's location.

Only two notable problems appeared in the Models S in its first year of production. First, the small 12 volt accessory battery was starting to exhibit reliability problems in some cars. With Tesla's remote diagnostics, they could often tell if the battery was about to fail. Tesla would then proactively schedule a service call. It turns out the battery was sourced from a reputable American company, who unbeknownst to Tesla, was outsourced to a Chinese company, who then sourced it from a Vietnamese company! The quality was not up to Tesla's standards, and while not an urgent issue, Tesla replaced all those batteries regardless.

The only recall on the Model S to date has been for a weld joint on the back seat that was not up to Tesla standards. Tesla discovered the problem occurred during four weeks of production in May 2013. Even though no one complained or was even aware of the issue, Tesla voluntarily issued a recall to inspect and repair if needed. For this recall, they took a loaner Model S to the customer's desired location, repaired and returned the owner's car a few hours later.

Compare this with the more common manufacturer practice of ignoring problems until either the National Traffic and Safety Administration forces a recall, or only after enough people are hurt that the legal expense and bad publicity outweighs the recall costs. Tesla's policy is to design and produce to excessively high quality and reliability standards. Should a problem occur, Tesla is thoughtful, honest, and proactive with its customers.

Reliability Path

# Warranty

Tesla provides a unique warranty that raises the bar for other luxury car makers. The primary warranty runs for 4 years or 50,000 miles, whichever comes first. This is a bumper-to-bumper type warranty that covers everything except abuse and tires. Even brakes, wiper blades and lights are included.

Tesla's battery pack warranty exceeds other car makers when it comes to mileage. The battery pack gets an additional warranty from defects or failure for 8 years or 125,000 miles in the 60 kWh model, and 8 years unlimited miles in the 85 kWh models. While Tesla has some basic care guidelines for charging the battery, the battery warranty remains in effect even if these guidelines are not followed. For example, should the battery pack fail because an owner completely drains the battery, Tesla replaces the battery pack under warranty free of charge. In general, Tesla's battery pack warranty covers everything except in the case of deliberate damage or damage from a car crash.

Tesla recommends that the Model S have an inspection every year or every 12,500 miles, but this is optional. Even improper maintenance does not invalidate the warranty. Tesla's faith in its product quality allows them to offer one of the best warranty programs. Model S owners have the assurance that they may never have to incur the cost of replacing a battery pack given the average length of ownership.

## Cool Fact

Long term testing on the battery pack has exceeded the equivalent of 500,000 miles!

# Worth the Wait

At Tesla, customers select the attributes of the Model S that matter most to them – range, color, decor, and options. Then Tesla builds each car to order. In the United States, delivery usually takes between one to three months. Tesla believes customers who buy a premium car deserve personalization, even if that entails a short wait.

## But I want it NOW!

Tesla recognizes that some customers want a car immediately. For these customers, Tesla makes a small number of preconfigured Model S cars. When available, a preconfigured car is bought and driven away immediately. Uniform pricing prevails regardless even if it's an immediate purchase, but the customer does not get the opportunity to select specific options.

Long before the factory started producing the Model S, Tesla took reservations starting in March 2009. Those early customers made refundable deposits of $40,000 to get one of the first 1000 Signature editions that offered special options such as white leather and Signature red paint. Other customers put down $5,000 and were put in the queue after the Signature reservations. When those reservations were made, no firm production date existed. Those customers ended up waiting three to four years to get their car. So today's average waiting period of one to three months seems quite reasonable in comparison especially since these are customized, built-to-order cars.

> ### Cool Fact
> Tesla's build-to-order strategy avoids huge inventory carrying costs, helping to lower the vehicle cost.

The Model S is so popular that customers around the world are still willing to wait. Although delivery began in the summer of 2012 to U.S. customers, it took another year for Tesla to start deliveries to reservation holders in Europe. Some of the delay is attributed to country specific requirements, such as right-hand drive. As it becomes certified in each country and meets other business requirements, wait times should decrease quickly.

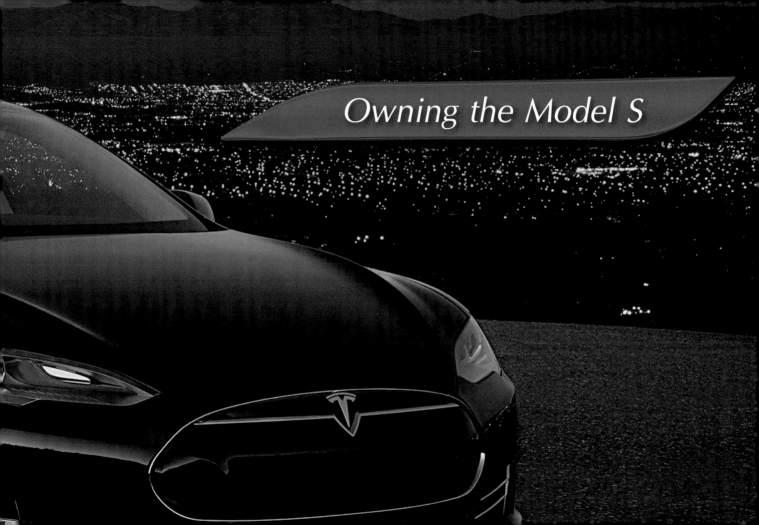

*Owning the Model S*

# Tips and Tricks

If you have time-of-day electric rates where you charge, set the charge timer to start charging at the lowest cost of the day, typically starting at midnight.

Some functions are GPS location aware. For example, if you manually reduce the default charging current, it remembers the value for that location. The time-of-day charge setting and Homelink functions are also location aware.

After adjusting the driver's seat, steering wheel driving position and side mirrors, tap the person icon at the top of the display to save these memory positions in your driver profile. Up to ten personal profiles are stored here (requires Tech Package).

A light press up or down on the turn-signal stalk activates the turn-signal for three flashes.

While in the car, to extend the door handles to let a passenger in, press park.

In Controls (lower-left Touchscreen button) spend a few minutes going through every setting for each Tab to select the operations you prefer.

Set the side mirrors to tilt downwards when backing up. With the car in Reverse, adjust the mirrors to the desired position. Save the settings by tapping the person icon in the top line of the main display. Once set, every time you go into reverse, the mirrors tilt downward to give you a better view of possible obstructions (requires Tech Package, although some early cars without Tech Package have this feature too).

The first time you bring your car home, test to make sure the hatchback liftgate doesn't open too high and hit the ceiling or garage door. Hold on to the liftgate as you manually open it and stop when it's at the correct height, press and hold the liftgate button for five seconds to lock in the desired height (requires Tech Package).

When the weather is hot, at first the A/C may make a slightly louder hum as the HVAC runs at the maximum power for a minute or two to cool down the cabin. This is normal.

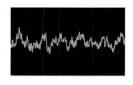

Try out the left and right steering scroll wheels to see what they do. Press inward to make a selection. A long press changes what appears on the left and right sides of the instrument display.

The J1772 charging adapter stores in the glove box. It fits perfectly in a deep recess on the left side.

If you need a tow, insist on a flatbed tow truck and be sure to check the manual or pamphlet in the glove box for towing

instructions. An improper tow may seriously damage the battery and lead to a very expensive repair bill.

The Google map accepts pinch and zoom gestures or slide the map with a finger. To return the center to your current

position, tap the white gear icon near the top-left of the pane.

Tap the blue lightning bolt in the top-right of this pane to display a red icon at Super-chargers and last charging point locations. If you have the Tech Package, tap the red icon to quickly navigate to that location.

On the FOB, press the center 'roof' button for 5 seconds to roll down all the windows.

When navigating to a location, the small navigation overlay on the main display shows upcoming actions.

This list is scrollable if there are more than three actions remaining.

Tap on an action and the map centers on that location. Tap again to return to the prior state (requires Tech Package).

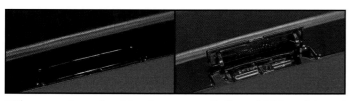

When equipped with the sunroof, four hidden hinged mounting points allow attachment of a roof rack and accessories to carry bikes and other gear on the roof.

AAA has a charging truck they can dispatch to EVs in some areas should you run out of power. They supply a 10-15 minute 240V quick charge via the J1772 adapter. This should be enough to reach a nearby charging station.

Cars with leather seats have extra pouches most owners are not aware of. You find it at the very front of the seat bottom.

Air vents are closed off by sliding the lever to the far left on the driver's side, and far right on the passenger's side.

Each door has a small storage area as part of the door pull to store your keys or other small items.

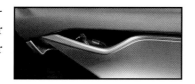

To hear the ultimate in music quality, save songs in lossless FLAC or lossless WMA to a USB flash drive. If you have the Ultra High Fidelity Sound option, turn off Dolby 7.1 for enhanced music quality.

# Wild Customizations

Like most luxury sports cars, after-market customizations abound on the Model S.

Some of the cool modifications shown on this page include rear-seat video displays with DVD player, blind-spot warning system, integrated radar detector, audio enhancements, and trunk lighting; all installed by Al & Ed's Autosound.

Other more common modifications and accessories cover sub-woofers (*left*), wheels, frunk lighting, center consoles, tow hitches, paint armor, window tinting, dash-cams, and more!

Shown on the right is a cool blue wrapped car with Vossen Wheels matte graphite 22" Concave CV1 wheels and carbon fiber accents. Car wraps are a clever way to change the color or add a pattern printed on a vinyl and applied to the car. The original color is restored by removing the wrap as it does not hurt the paint.

**Cool Fact**

Some owners have spent over $20,000 in after market customizations!

# Service with a Smile

Tesla builds and operates its own group of service centers for all warranty and repair work. This is a growing network with over 50 centers at the start of 2014.

Initially an annual servicing was required in order to preserve warranty coverage. But as CEO Elon Musk conceded this mandatory requirement was quickly dropped given that the car doesn't even need an oil change. Even though it's optional, Tesla still recommends an annual service checkup. Extended service plans are available that vary by cost depending on the number of years, number of miles, and whether Tesla Ranger service is included.

In the event a service is expected to take more than four hours, Tesla provides a free loaner car. Tesla stocks service centers with top-of-the-line P85 Model S cars and some Tesla Roadster loaners. They even offer a trade-in option for the loaner if you like it better than your own car!

For an additional fee, ranger service is available. With this service, a ranger technician performs most servicing needs at the customer's work or home.

In a very unusual business decision, Tesla stated that service is not a profit center. Typically in a dealership, service and parts is the most profitable portion of the business, with gross margins typically above 50%. Also unusual for service, Tesla technicians and service writers are not on commission. This policy avoids conflict of interests and ensures that customer satisfaction remains the top priority for all Tesla service personnel.

### Cool Fact
Technicians work safely indoors in closed areas, since there are no poisonous carbon monoxide emissions from Tesla vehicles.

*Fremont, California Service Bay*

# Missing Parts

An ICE car has numerous parts that are unnecessary in a Tesla electric vehicle. With the Model S, you never have to worry about these parts failing or wearing out and leaving you stranded. You'll enjoy the lower maintenance costs and the higher reliability of a Model S!

Just imagine no longer having to deal with periodic oil and filter changes and annoying smog tests. No more replacing spark-plugs, timing belts, and mufflers. Check out our partial list of the hundreds of parts you won't miss having on your Model S (*right*).

### Cool Fact

Many ICE engines use an interference design. If the timing belt breaks, the engine is destroyed when pistons push into opened valves. This can occur in milliseconds without any warning.

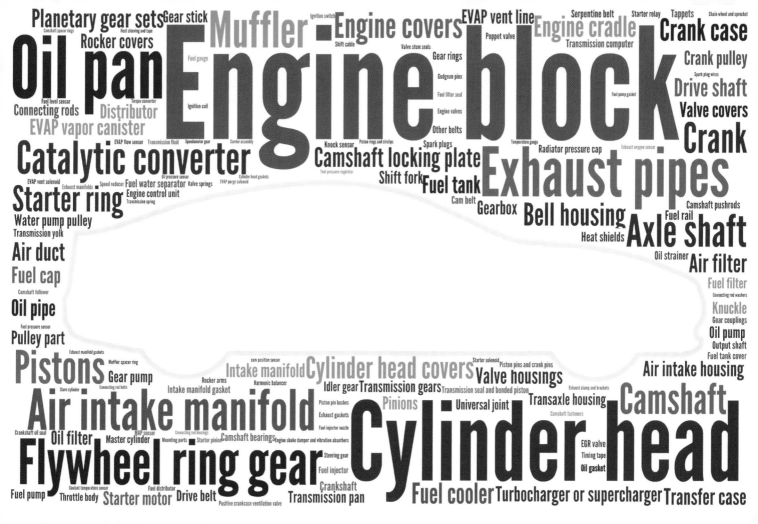

# The Fans

Tesla fans range from enthusiastic owners, reservation holders and those who love the car, but can't afford or quite pull the trigger yet. The group invokes similar passions that only a handful of other cars receive, such as the Chevrolet Corvette and Porsche 911. Cars only create this kind of fervor when the vehicles offer a clear and dramatic improvement that change the way people think about transportation.

Fans have created a number of Tesla Motors websites (including the author's own TeslaTap.com site) that cover forums, blogs, advice, polls, news, modifications and much more. A number of these sites began before the Model S shipped! A few customers even created studio quality commercials showing off the Model S.

The first Tesla fan-based convention, Teslive, occurred in Fremont, California in July 2013. The entire event was organized by fans for fans, with exhibitors, seminars, talks, fun drives and more. Elon Musk and JB Straubel were keynote speakers and answered many attendee questions. Tesla Motors also gave factory tours and hosted the nighttime party at the factory. In all, it was a huge success and planning is underway for next year's event.

Another fan event is the annual Tour De Tesla's Southern California Tesla Run. Around 125 Tesla Model S and Roadster owners gathered at the Hawthorne Design Studio/Supercharger station.

Tesla treated participants to a delicious breakfast while everyone got registered. We then took off around the Los Angeles freeways guided by a team of 12 officers on motorcycles. The long caravan of Teslas was quite a sight! At one point they closed off Highway 5 (a major three lane freeway) so the group could stay together and get onto the freeway. We ended the 31 mile run at the famous Petersen Automobile Museum.

Tesla owners are one of the best free sales force a company could have. They enthusiastically introduce Tesla's groundbreaking new technology to friends and neighbors. Car parties with test drives around the block often occur as soon as new owners get their car. Everyone wants to see the car, even strangers stop and ask about the Model S.

Car manufacturers frequently give cars away to celebrities to promote their car but that's not necessary for Tesla. VIPs have actually paid full price to get their hands on their own Model S.

*GM's 1997 EV1 at the Petersen Automobile Museum*

### Cool Fact

Some well known names that have bought a Model S include Ben Affleck, Cameron Diaz, Laurence Fishburne, Morgan Freeman, Steven Spielberg, and Steve Wozniak.

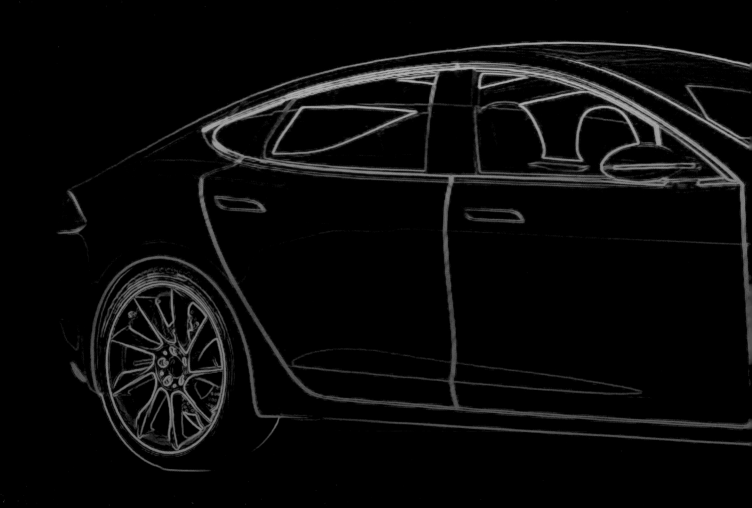

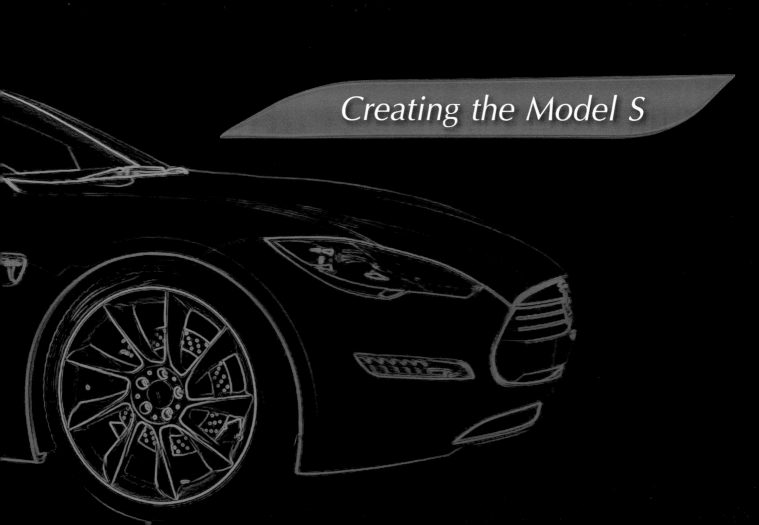

Creating the Model S

# WhiteStar

Tesla began planning for additional cars in its lineup even before the Roadster was in production. While the Roadster proved the technology in a low-volume, two-seater car, the next model aimed to appeal to a broader group of people. This new model would be a medium volume car at half the cost. It would compete with mid-range luxury sedans, costing $41,000 to $52,000 in today's dollars.

By the end of 2006, Tesla went public with this 4-door, 5 passenger sedan project, code-named WhiteStar. Even at this early phase, they planned for a rear-mounted motor with a battery mounted in the floor.

Tesla contracted with Fisker Coachbuild for exterior and interior styling work on WhiteStar at the start of 2007. Fisker was already selling re-skinned BMW and Mercedes-Benz cars and providing contracting services to other vehicle companies.

Tesla also announced the opening of a design and development center in Rochester Hills, just north of Detroit for future products, starting with the WhiteStar sports sedan. By August 2007, 35 Tesla engineers were working in Michigan on the WhiteStar project.

During the WhiteStar development, Fisker created a joint venture with Quantum at the start of 2008. This venture was formed to create and build a new high-end hybrid sports car that was to become the Fisker Karma. While Tesla's contracts didn't prohibit developing a competitive product, Tesla felt that Fisker had taken confidential

### Cool Fact

During its very early design stage, Tesla seriously considered making the WhiteStar a plug-in hybrid. Fortunately they discarded this idea to focus only on electric vehicles.

engineering designs and used Tesla's strategic business plan in creating the Karma. Tesla then fired Fisker Coachbuild and in April 2008, sued them for trade secret theft.

Elon Musk told the New York Times, "The styling was substandard compared to what he unveiled for his product. He gave us an inferior work product, and it's obvious why." In the end, Fisker prevailed with no evidence Fisker used any Tesla confidential information. Tesla elected to dump the Fisker designs, and start over, losing considerable development time. Fisker successfully slowed Tesla and had a free look at everything Tesla was doing. Of course, now that Fisker went bankrupt, it goes to show that sometimes the good guys like Tesla do win out!

In August 2008, Tesla hired Franz von Holzhausen as the Chief Designer away from Mazda, where he designed the RX8. The WhiteStar development was once again rapidly moving forward.

*WhiteStar design concept sculpted in clay*

# Prototypes

Tesla first unveiled the Model S to the press at the SpaceX factory in March 2009. Contrary to most manufacturer's prototypes, almost all of the exterior design shape was retained in the production car.

Changes between the prototype and production cars included removing the cool blue daylight running lights, a color not legal in the USA. Other tweaks were made to the lower front fascia with openings added for small HVAC radiators at each side; puddle lights were moved from the side mirrors to the undersides of the doors; the side light style changed; and a chrome trim was added at the bottom rear. The charging port was changed from a gas cap style to one hidden in the rear brake light assembly. Interior dash styling also changed quite a bit. The dramatic all digital cockpit with its 17" touch screen display was retained.

Of the first two prototype cars made, one was a non-running shell, and the other a fully driveable version. These were introduced publicly at Tesla's Menlo Park showroom in March 2009, where they gave short test drives and began taking refundable deposit reservations.

## Cool Fact

After building the prototypes, Tesla built 20 alpha Model S's to shake out safety, durability, manufacturability, electronics, performance and handling.

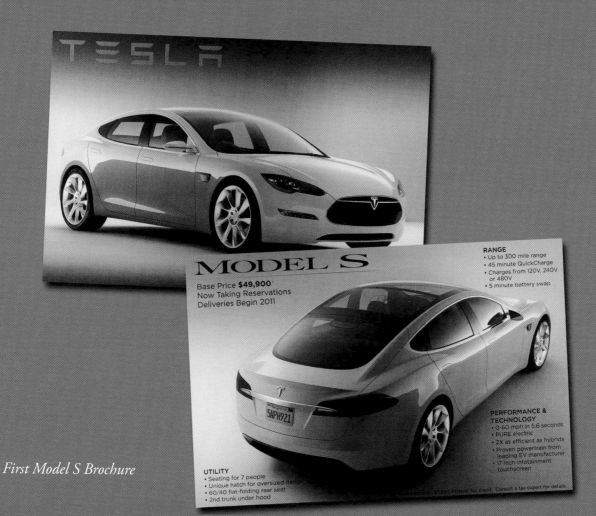

*First Model S Brochure*

# TESLA

## MODEL S

Base Price **$49,900**[*]
Now Taking Reservations
Deliveries Begin 2011

**RANGE**
- Up to 300 mile range
- 45 minute QuickCharge
- Charges from 120V, 240V or 480V
- 5 minute battery swap

**PERFORMANCE & TECHNOLOGY**
- 0-60 mph in 5.6 seconds
- PURE electric
- 2X as efficient as hybrids
- Proven powertrain from leading EV manufacturer
- 17 inch infotainment touchscreen

**UTILITY**
- Seating for 7 people
- Unique hatch for oversized items
- 60/40 flat-folding rear seat
- 2nd trunk under hood

# Factories

Tesla produces the Model S at its Fremont, California factory. The factory was previously the NUMMI (New United Motors Manufacturing) plant, jointly owned by GM and Toyota. In its 27 years of operation, it produced vehicles such as the Pontiac Vibe and Toyota Corolla. As a result of the drastic industry downturn in 2009, GM discontinued production of the Pontiac Vibe at the plant and pulled out of the joint venture. On April 1, 2010, Toyota also ceased its manufacturing operations at the Fremont plant.

Tesla and Toyota announced their own joint deal in May 2010. Tesla paid Toyota $42 million for the 5.2 million-square-foot NUMMI factory with 207 acres of land. In addition, Toyota agreed to invest $50 million in exchange for Tesla common stock. In retrospect, it was undoubtedly a great deal for Tesla and Toyota. Tesla further expanded the property in the summer of 2013 with the acquisition of the adjacent 35 acres of land that was previously leased for their test track.

*NUMMI Factory, East view, 2010*

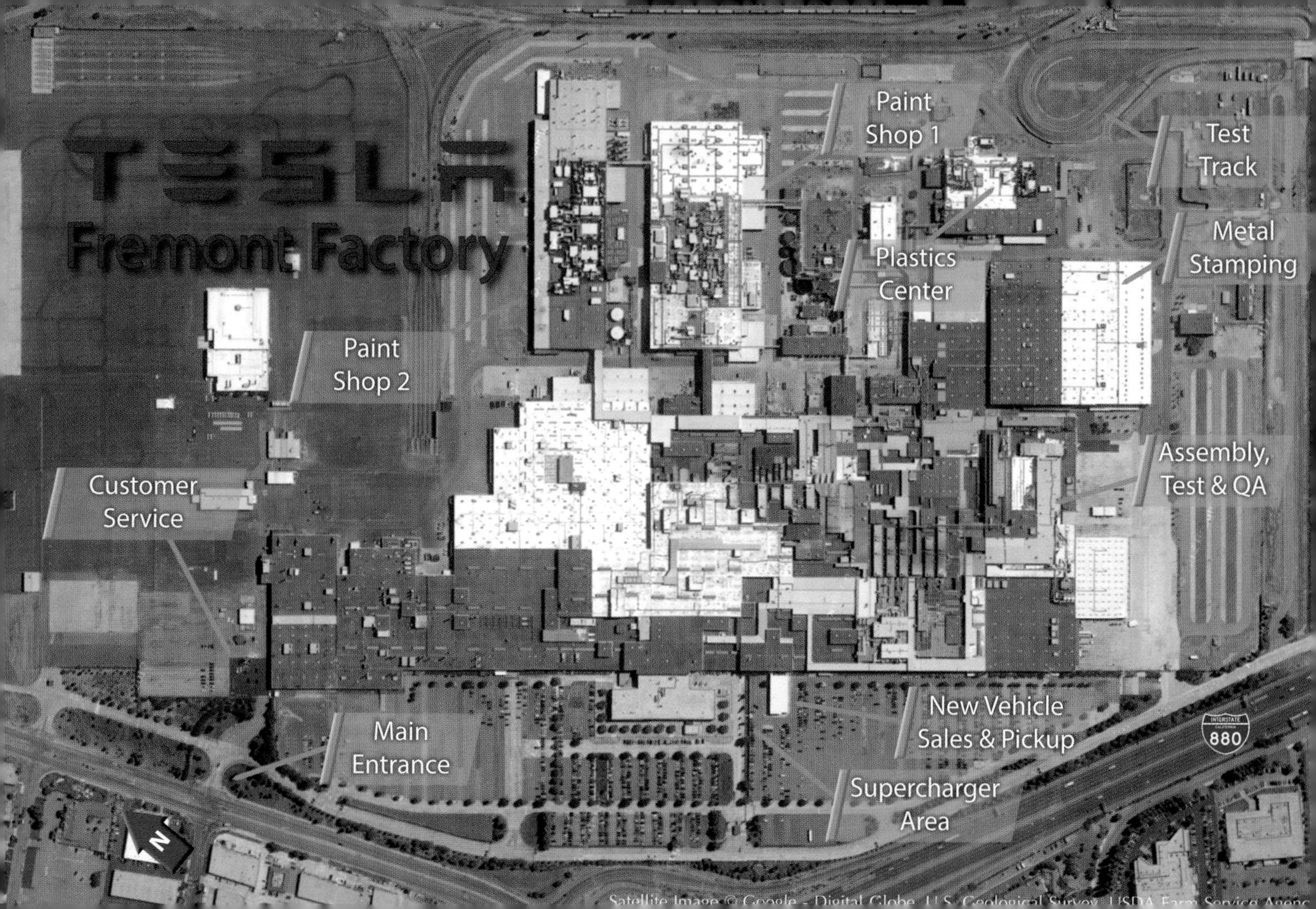

TESLA
Fremont Factory

Paint Shop 1

Test Track

Metal Stamping

Plastics Center

Paint Shop 2

Assembly, Test & QA

Customer Service

New Vehicle Sales & Pickup

Main Entrance

Supercharger Area

INTERSTATE 880

Satellite Image © Google - Digital Globe, U.S. Geological Survey, USDA Farm Service Agency

Tesla rebuilt portions of the factory by converting the old dirty, grimy factory floor into a clean white assembly area. Taking advantage of the recession, Tesla bought key factory equipment at bargain prices from distressed auto companies, such as the massive Schuler SMG hydraulic stamping-press, valued at $50 million, but purchased for only $6 million. At the same time, Tesla upgraded the factory with the latest robotics to speed the assembly process. Tesla's factory cost approximately $59 million for plant, land, and equipment that is now estimated to be worth over a billion dollars.

The factory run rate is over 30,000 cars annually at the start of 2014. During GM and Toyota's 2006 peak year, the NUMMI factory produced over 428,600 cars and trucks. So, Tesla's factory can easily accommodate future expansion for years to come.

*Tesla's Taiwan Factory*

Tesla's Taiwan factory produces the motors and inverters. Light manufacturing is also performed at Tesla's Palo Alto headquarters, such as components for Superchargers.

*Tesla Fremont Factory, North view, 2013*

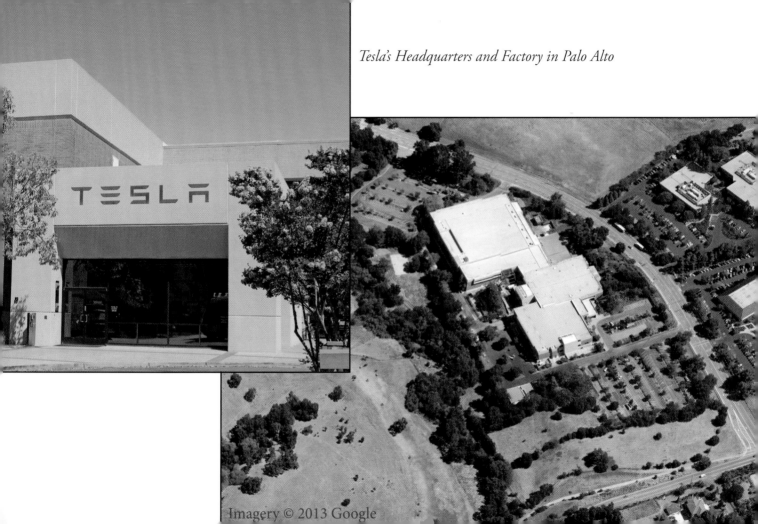

*Tesla's Headquarters and Factory in Palo Alto*

Imagery © 2013 Google

# How to Make a Car

Building the Model S requires over 3000 factory workers running multiple production shifts and more than 150 multi-tasking robots. Vehicles take three to five days to build starting from the raw materials. Our factory tour guides you through many of the key steps in making the Model S at Tesla's state-of-the-art Fremont, California factory.

## Metal Stamping

The Model S frame starts with coils of aluminum sheeting from Alcoa. These coils are delivered in different widths and alloys depending on requirements of the final part. A single coil weighs up to 20,000 pounds and costs over $40,000 each. An overhead bridge crane lifts the desired coil into place.

The aluminum from the coils is unfurled and cut into rectangles called 'blanks' based on the size of the part to be made. Lasers may be used to cut the smaller blanks while larger parts are stamped into shape.

For the largest parts, blanks are robotically fed into the Schuler five-station transfer press line.

The Schuler hydraulic press line forms, trims and pierces the blank in multiple sequential steps to create a final aluminum part, such as a hood, door or side frame. The press line can produce a part every six seconds!

While hard to tell in the photo, the press line is seven stories tall, with 3 stories below the floor's surface. It is the largest hydraulic press in North America, and the 6th largest in the world.

To the left are four sets of dies that are used to make a part. These are installed in the press for a run of parts, or swapped out for a different set of dies to make a different part.

A single die weighs up to 80,000 pounds (32,000 kg). Typically four sets of dies are used to make one part. In some cases, a die set makes a group of parts at the same time. For example, the left and right door panels are made at the same time with a single die set.

The right side aluminum structure is one of many parts created on-site for the Model S.

## Body Framing Shop

The underbody structure is assembled first and becomes the frame for the rest of the body.

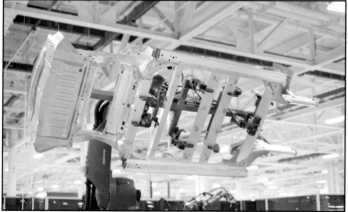

Metal parts are attached to the aluminum side structure for additional rollover protection.

On the Body Framing Line, robots pick up the aluminum side structure assembly and fit it onto the underbody frame (*left*).

Other assemblies are added along the line. Robots join parts using one of five methods: industrial-strength adhesive bonding, spot welding, resistance welding, cold metal transfer welding, or self-piercing riveting (*right*).

Once framed, lasers measure key holes and gaps to 0.1mm to confirm the assembly meets quality objectives.

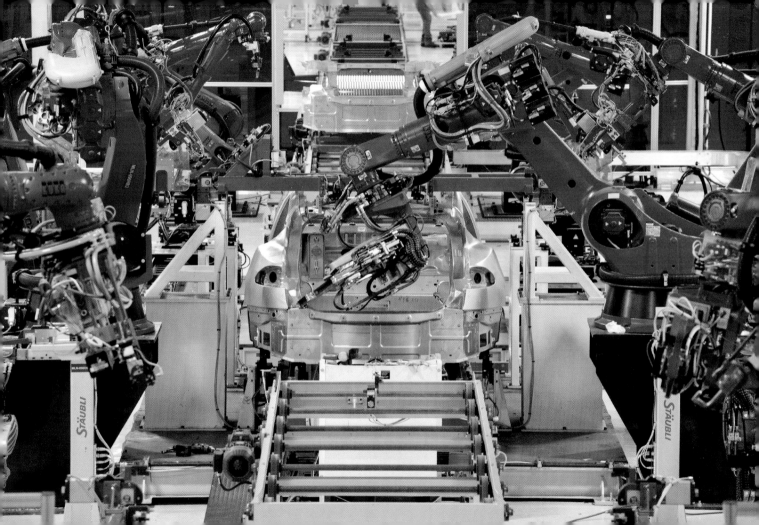

The doors, hood and hatch sub-assemblies are attached. This assembly is called the "body-in-white", indicating it is ready for painting. It is robotically lifted onto an overhead conveyor, where it moves to the paint shop.

## Paint Shop

To ensure a perfect car finish, robots perform the entire paint process in an absolute clean environment. In the Paint Center, the "body-in-white" is first submerged in a pre-treatment bath. Next it's submerged in an electro-coating solution to place a continuous, low-profile film over the entire vehicle's surface to protect against corrosion. The film is baked on at 350° F.

A sealer is applied into critical seams of the car to make the underbody waterproof and quiet.

Robotic sprayers apply a powder primer coat. The doors, hood, and trunk are opened by robots to paint all areas of the vehicle.

After the primer is oven dried, the body is moved to one of 10 paint lines – one for each color Tesla offers. The color coat is robotically applied and then oven dried.

For multi-coat paints, a second color coat solution is sprayed on after the first color coat has dried to get a luscious depth and glow.

Lastly, a powder clear coat layer is applied and oven dried.

After the paint is dry, the car is wet sanded by hand. Each car is carefully inspected in a brightly lit room to ensure a perfect paint job. The paint process takes about one and a half days from start to finish.

## Parts Warehouse

One of many aisles in the massive parts storage area holds assemblies, outsourced parts, and internally made parts. Parts from the storage area are sent to the final assembly area.

This area looks reminiscent of the final warehouse image in the Raiders of the Lost Ark movie!

## Final Assembly

The newly painted frame is placed onto a SmartCart. It then moves through the final assembly area by following a magnetic path on the floor. The SmartCart allows factory workers to raise and lower the body, making it easier to work on the car.

Should a problem develop on a single car that can't be solved quickly, the SmartCart is easily moved out of the line, preventing an expensive line stoppage.

The doors are temporarily removed and attached to stations on the SmartCart for better access to the car's interior and doors.

The production crew installs and routes the wiring harness throughout the car.

For vehicles with the panoramic sunroof option, a robot lifts and places the glass sunroof onto the top of the body. High-definition 3D cameras ensure the placement is perfect (*left*).

High-voltage wiring, mechanical components such as the steering, pedals and duct work are installed (*bottom*).

The interior surfaces, seats, dashboard and door panels are manufactured by FUTURiS. They rent a portion of the Tesla factory floor near the assembly area to make the needed components on demand.

A robotic arm places a front passenger seat into position. The protective cover on the seat is removed before delivery (*left*).

After the seats, dashboard and interior trim are installed, the doors are attached (*bottom*).

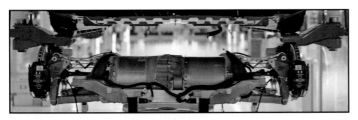

The electric motor, transaxle, inverter, and rear suspension system are built into a single rear sub-assembly elsewhere in the factory. This rear sub-assembly along with the front suspension assembly are lifted into the car.

Robots assemble the battery pack in an upper floor of the factory. The finished four-inch thick pack is lifted and bolted into place.

The battery and powertrain components are connected while the car hangs from an overhead lift (*right*).

The bumper fascias are molded and painted in the Plastics Center. Depending on the options ordered on the car, fog lamps, lower lighting modules, parking sensors and related wiring are all installed to complete the fascia sub-assemblies. The fascias are then moved to final assembly (*not shown*).

The final assembly steps include installing the boron steel bumpers, bumper fascia assemblies, and emblems.

Wheels are attached and all five lug nuts are tightened at the same time.

## Final Inspection

With the assembly complete, the car is powered up for the first time. At this stage, the car goes through a long list of inspections, tests and checks to confirm that the car is working perfectly.

Visual inspections are performed on a bamboo floor to ensure a perfect fit and finish.

The headlights are adjusted and the suspension is aligned. Next, the car is moved to the dynamometer. The car's motor, suspension, and brakes are tested under various simulated driving conditions.

To verify correct suspension operation under different surface conditions, cars used to be driven on an indoor test track (*left*). With the increase in production, these tests are now performed outside after the water test.

Each car is placed in a glass high-pressure water test booth. Then, 228 jets spray water on the exterior. QA inspectors verify there are no leaks (*left*).

Water for the test booth is stored in a 1500 gallon tank. It is purified and re-used for each test to conserve resources.

The test track adjacent to the factory confirms proper operation on the road (*bottom*).

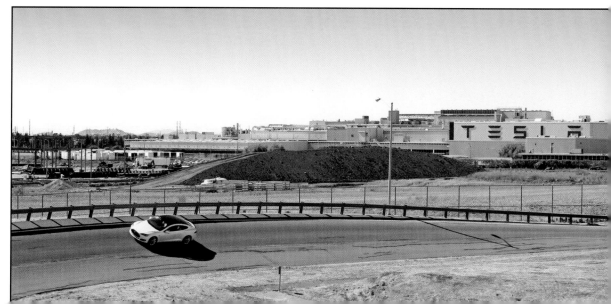

## Delivery

Each car gets a wash, charge and per-delivery inspection. The completed car is now ready for delivery (bottom).

The Model S is shipped to a Tesla showroom, service center or the Fremont factory for customer pick up (*right*).

On delivery, the Tesla Delivery Specialist reviews the car's operation and answers questions for the new owner. If you pick up the car at the factory, you'll also get a free guided factory tour!

# Innovations

Tesla's business and technical innovations impress everyone from auto reviewers to customers. No wonder Tesla has received so many awards. Here's a highlight of Tesla's best innovations from the Roadster and Model S that are revolutionizing the car industry.

## Business Innovations

- First successful publicly traded car company in America in more than 50 years

- Cars purchased over the Internet instead of through dealers

- Showrooms located in convenient customer locations such as shopping malls

- Completely transparent pricing, no rebates, MSRP or dealer invoice prices, single pricing for all

- Tesla doesn't have any sales people. Tesla's Product Specialists are non-commissioned, making for a stress free learning environment at their showrooms

- Service is not a profit center, so service is aligned with customer's best interests

- No paid advertising, using customers, social media and media events to spread the news

- Cars are built to order which allows you to get exactly what you want

- Supercharger network provides free long-distance traveling

- Designed core technology in-house resulting in cost savings and performance advantages

## Technical Innovations for Production Vehicles

- First auto maker with high performance zero-emission cars

- Elimination of the transmission simplifies the design and provides instant response

- Use of a great many, small, custom designed, cost-efficient lithium-ion cells in the battery pack

- Built in charger allows charging anywhere

- Battery pack with superior HVAC system extends battery life, boosts performance, safety and reliability

- Technology for a 90 second battery swapping system

- Digital motor controller instead of analog for improved reliability and smoothness

- High definition 17" touch-screen display for infotainment and navigation

- Future enhancements with wireless software updates

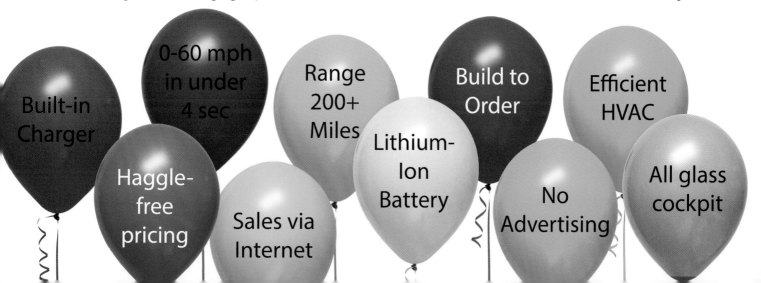

# The Tesla Story

Tesla Motors, named after the AC induction motor inventor Nikola Tesla, is one of those rare companies that comes along and disrupts an established industry. Founded in 2003, Tesla has focused on three goals:

- Produce a range of car models, each one being the absolute best in its class proving that all-electric vehicles are more desirable than comparable ICE cars

- Make each generation of EVs more affordable than the last, bringing clean energy transport to the masses to accelerate the move from a petroleum-based economy to a sustainable energy economy

- Develop and sell electric powertrain technology to other companies to speed release of their own EVs

Tesla's first car was the Roadster, a two-seater sports car. It blew away all previous complaints about electric cars being slow, ugly and range limited. Instead, it delivers an incredible EPA range of 244 miles per charge, zips along easily at 130 mph, and accelerates from 0-60 mph in 3.9 seconds. It stunned the market by being so much better than its ICE rivals. The Roadster even looked great, something unexpected from a new company, let alone an electric car!

To bring the Roadster to market faster, Tesla worked with Group Lotus, experts in low volume vehicle production. While Tesla planned to use the Lotus Elise as the base platform to reduce the design work, Tesla heavily modified the frame, created all new carbon fiber body panels, and created the entire drivetrain. In the end, less than 7% of the Elise parts were retained in the Roadster. With the design complete, Group Lotus was contracted to assemble "gliders," the Roadster shell without the electric powertrain.

Tesla Incorporated by founders, Martin Eberhard, CEO and Marc Tarpenning, CFO
Jul-2003

 Ian Wright joins as VP of Vehicle Development and founder
Jan-2004

 Elon Musk becomes investor, Chairman of the Board and founder; $7.5 million Series A Investment Round
Apr-2004

 JB Straubel joins as the Chief Technology Officer and final founder
May-2004

 Primary styling of Roadster created by Barney Hatt
Dec-2004

$13 Million Series B Investment round
Feb-2005

 Roadster packaging & visualizations complete
Mar-2005

 Tesla signs production contract with Lotus Group for Roadster gliders
Jul-2005

$40 Million Series C Investment round
May-2006

 Roadster officially launched; Test-drives with the first two Engineering Prototypes (EP)
Jul-2006

 Elon Musk announces plan for future lower-cost EV cars (what will become the Model S)
Aug-2006

 First Auto Show - Showing EP2 at San Francisco
Nov-2006

2003

2004

2005

2006

The base price of the Roadster started at $109,000. Tesla sold over 2400 Roadsters in over 35 countries during its production run from 2008 to 2012. Along the way the Roadster received numerous awards worldwide.

A few years before the Roadster went into production, Tesla started work on their second EV, the Model S. This would be a much higher volume, premium 4-door sport sedan, at half the price of the Roadster. Unlike the Roadster, Tesla designed the Model S from the ground up to take advantage of their electric powertrain technology.

Tesla unveiled the Model S prototype in March 2009 to the press and public. The car was dramatically better than anyone had imagined! Potential customers took a short ride as passengers, in the only functioning Model S prototype. Within a week, Tesla received 500 deposits from enthusiastic consumers.

Going from prototype to full-scale production turned out to be incredibly difficult. Besides solving difficult technological problems - financial, manufacturing, and business hurdles also threatened to derail Tesla. Many in the industry and the press expected Tesla to go bankrupt long before any cars rolled off its assembly line. Even Elon Musk admitted that starting a car company cost at least five times more than he had anticipated.

Established auto makers typically spend a few billion dollars and five years to design and deliver a new car. These auto makers have many advantages over tiny upstart Tesla. They often reuse parts from prior designs. They also have a large staff of designers, engineers, managers, sales, marketing, factories, supply chains, and more!

In contrast, Tesla spent around $500 million and less than five years to develop the Model S. Getting the Model S into production required Tesla to create an infrastructure to manufacture, sell and service the Model S. A factory was bought and outfitted. Sales galleries and service centers were built and staffed. All this with many nay-sayers constantly braying it couldn't be done!

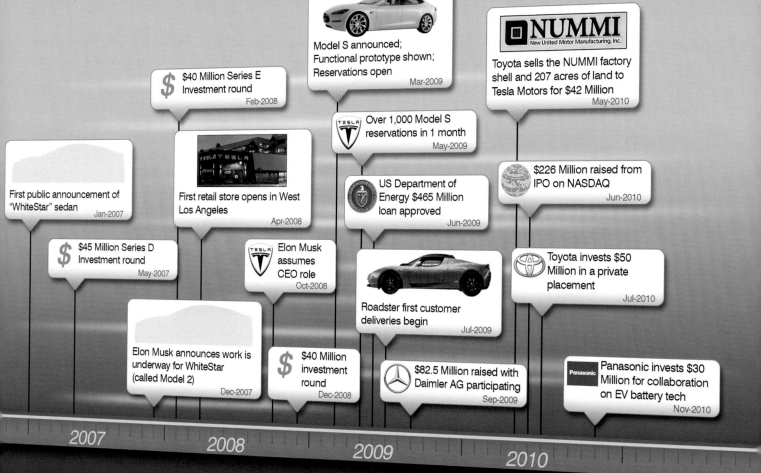

First public announcement of "WhiteStar" sedan
Jan-2007

$45 Million Series D Investment round
May-2007

Elon Musk announces work is underway for WhiteStar (called Model 2)
Dec-2007

$40 Million Series E Investment round
Feb-2008

First retail store opens in West Los Angeles
Apr-2008

Elon Musk assumes CEO role
Oct-2008

$40 Million investment round
Dec-2008

Model S announced; Functional prototype shown; Reservations open
Mar-2009

Over 1,000 Model S reservations in 1 month
May-2009

US Department of Energy $465 Million loan approved
Jun-2009

Roadster first customer deliveries begin
Jul-2009

$82.5 Million raised with Daimler AG participating
Sep-2009

NUMMI
New United Motor Manufacturing, Inc.
Toyota sells the NUMMI factory shell and 207 acres of land to Tesla Motors for $42 Million
May-2010

$226 Million raised from IPO on NASDAQ
Jun-2010

Toyota invests $50 Million in a private placement
Jul-2010

Panasonic invests $30 Million for collaboration on EV battery tech
Nov-2010

2007　　2008　　2009　　2010

As an EV auto maker, Tesla continued to overcome unique challenges, such as: sourcing enough lithium-ion battery production, addressing customer range anxiety by creating a network of charging stations called Superchargers, and neutralizing efforts to prohibit Tesla from selling cars in various states.

Despite these challenges and potential roadblocks, Tesla began limited deliver of the Model S in June 2012. It continues to have a waiting list even with a few small price increases. Delivery outside of North America began in August 2013 starting in Europe with the first Model S delivered to Oslo, Norway. Just like the Roadster, the Model S has received numerous awards.

Tesla introduced their third all-electric prototype, the Model X, a large crossover sport utility vehicle, in February 2012. The Model X is designed for families who need lots of storage space and three rows of front facing seats that comfortably seats seven adults. Most striking about this car are its rear "falcon-wing" futuristic-looking doors.

Tesla plans to start production of the Model X at the end of 2014. I expect pricing to be similar to the Model S even though it's a bigger car with undoubtedly awesome new technologies yet to be revealed!

Tesla has also begun work on an even lower cost, high volume car for the 2017-2018 time frame rumored to be called the Model E. It's targeted at a $35,000 price point. If Tesla follows its past pattern, the Model E prototype should be introduced in the same year the Model X starts production.

I expect the Model X and Model E will shake up the auto industry as has the Roadster and Model S. Tesla has clearly established a car brand that we count on to surprise, delight and exceed all our expectations.

### Cool Fact
Tesla's market cap now exceeds that of other vehicle manufacturers like Fiat and Mazda.

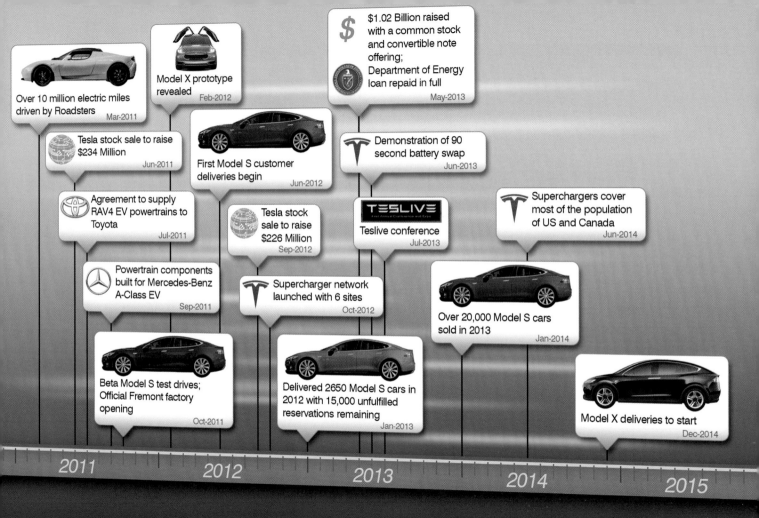

Over 10 million electric miles driven by Roadsters
Mar-2011

Model X prototype revealed
Feb-2012

$1.02 Billion raised with a common stock and convertible note offering; Department of Energy loan repaid in full
May-2013

Tesla stock sale to raise $234 Million
Jun-2011

First Model S customer deliveries begin
Jun-2012

Demonstration of 90 second battery swap
Jun-2013

Agreement to supply RAV4 EV powertrains to Toyota
Jul-2011

Tesla stock sale to raise $226 Million
Sep-2012

TESLIVE
First Annual Conference and Expo
Teslive conference
Jul-2013

Superchargers cover most of the population of US and Canada
Jun-2014

Powertrain components built for Mercedes-Benz A-Class EV
Sep-2011

Supercharger network launched with 6 sites
Oct-2012

Over 20,000 Model S cars sold in 2013
Jan-2014

Beta Model S test drives; Official Fremont factory opening
Oct-2011

Delivered 2650 Model S cars in 2012 with 15,000 unfulfilled reservations remaining
Jan-2013

Model X deliveries to start
Dec-2014

2011     2012     2013     2014     2015

# Locating Tesla

Tesla has numerous factories, offices, sales galleries, and service centers around the world. Many international offices were opened during the roll out of the Tesla Roadster. Tesla continues to expand at a rapid pace.

I created an extensive location time line and was quickly overwhelmed by the number of store and service center openings in 2013 and 2014. It would take more space than I thought it was worth, so the following timelines cover up through 2012. Needless to say, there are now many more stores and service centers than we've outlined here!

### Cool Fact

In 2007, the Model S factory was going to be built in Albuquerque, New Mexico. Plans changed in 2008. The factory would instead be located in San Jose due to a number of California state incentives.

Plans changed yet again when the Fremont NUMMI factory closed. Tesla bought the plant from Toyota in 2010 at a bargain price and now manufactures its Model S there.

# Locations

2003

**Menlo Park, California**
First Office

Jul-2003 to Jan-2004

2004

**San Carlos, California**
Headquarters

TESLA MOTORS

Feb-2004 to Jul-2009

**Norfolk, UK**
UK Office at Group Lotus

Feb-2005 to 2012

2005

2006

TESLA MOTORS

**San Chung City, Taiwan**
Motor Factory

Jul-2006

2007

**Rochester Hills, Michigan**
Development Facility

Jan-2007 to Oct-2008

**2008**

Menlo Park, California
Sales and Service

Jul-2008 to Oct-2013

West Los Angles, California
First Showroom
(Now only a Service Center)

May-2008

Palo Alto, California
Headquarters

Aug-2009

 London, England
Regional Sales & Service

Jun-2009

 New York, New York
Showroom

Jun-2009

 Seattle, Washington
Showroom

Jul-2009

 Munich, Germany
Showroom

Sep-2009

 Boulder, Colorado
Showroom

Oct-2009

 Chicago, Illinois
Showroom

Oct-2009

**2009**

 Monaco
Showroom

Nov-2009

 Dania Beach, Florida
Showroom

Dec-2009

 Newport Beach, California
Showroom

Jun-2010

 Copenhagen, Denmark
Showroom

Jun-2010

 Zurich, Switzerland
Showroom

Jun-2010

 Paris, France
Showroom

Sep-2010

**2010**

Fremont, California
NUMMI Factory Acquired

May-2010

 Los Angeles, California
Showroom

Dec-2010

 Tokyo, Japan
Showroom

Nov-2010

## 2011

**Toronto, Canada**
Showroom
Jan-2011

**Hawthorne, California**
Design Center
Estimated 2011

**Hong Kong**
Showroom
Aug-2011

**Houston, Texas**
Showroom
Oct-2011

**Milan, Italy**
Showroom
Feb-2011

**Washington, DC**
Showroom
Feb-2011

**San Jose, California**
Showroom
Apr-2011

**Lone Tree, Colorado**
Showroom
Jun-2011

**Eindhoven, Netherlands**
Showroom
Sep-2011

**Oak Brook, Illinois**
Showroom
Nov-2011

## 2012

**Oslo, Norway**
Showroom
Apr-2012

**Santa Monica, California**
Showroom
Jul-2012

**Scottsdale, Arizona**
Showroom
Jul-2012

**Portland, Oregon**
Showroom
Jul-2012

**Frankfurt, Germany**
Showroom
Aug-2012

**Tilburg, Netherlands**
Building acquired for final
assembly and European
Distribution Hub
Dec-2012

**White Plains, New York**
Showroom
May-2012

**Paramus, New Jersey**
Showroom
Sep-2012

**Garden City, New York**
Showroom
Sep-2012

**La Jolla, California**
Showroom
Oct-2012

**Skokie, Illinois**
Showroom
Oct-2012

**Natick, Massachusetts**
Showroom
Oct-2012

**Short Hills, New Jersey**
Showroom
Nov-2012

**Bellevue, Washington**
Showroom
Nov-2012

**Canoga Park, California**
Showroom
Nov-2012

**Miami Beach, Florida**
Showroom
Nov-2012

# Visionary Elon Musk

Elon Musk is a remarkable, technology entrepreneur with a highly successful, multi-company proven track record.

His first company, Zip2, started with his brother Kimbal Musk, provided online publishing software for large news organizations like the New York  Times and Hearst Publishing. After selling the company to Compaq, he created X.com for online financial services. He merged this with Confinity and co-founded PayPal, another big success that was later sold to eBay.

His interest in the possibility of space colonization led Elon Musk to create and fund his third company, Space X in 2002. He serves as its CEO and Chief Designer.

Space X designs, manufactures, and launches advanced rockets and spacecraft. Creating the first privately developed liquid-fueled rocket to reach orbit, they now handle cargo for the Space Station and launch orbital satellites.

Elon Musk always had a long standing interest in electric cars and promoting sustainable energy use. After a test drive in the AC Propulsion's tZero

prototype EV, he was convinced that electric cars with a good range were both possible to build, fun to drive, and desirable to own! With Martin Eberhard and Marc Tarpenning also looking at building a production EV based on the tZero, Elon joined the team as a co-founder, the Chairman of the Board, and principal investor.

**"The overarching goal of Tesla is to help reduce carbon emissions and that means low cost and high volume. We will also serve as an example to the auto industry, proving that the technology really works and customers want to buy electric vehicles."** *- Elon Musk*

Today, Elon Musk is Co-founder, Chairman, CEO and Product Architect of Tesla Motors. He assembled a great management team and attracted the best talent to work at Tesla Motors.

### Cool Fact
Elon Musk appears briefly in the movie *Iron Man 2*, as himself. In the movie he proposes an idea for an electric jet!

Elon also helped finance SolarCity and serves as its Chairman. His cousins, Lyndon and Peter Rive, founded SolarCi-

ty in 2006. SolarCity is one of the largest solar installers in the USA. They pioneered the solar leasing and power purchase agreement model where customers get solar installed without any direct costs. SolarCity also installs all the solar arrays on the Tesla Supercharger stations.

In August 2013, Elon felt compelled to propose a high-speed, Hyperloop transport system. The Hyperloop could transport people faster than an airplane and at a fraction the cost of California's proposed San Francisco to Los Angeles bullet train. Given California's budget woes, he urged Californians to consider better alternative solutions like the Hyperloop. Already too busy managing multiple companies, he challenged other entrepreneurs to advance his Hyperloop concept to reality. Indeed, he inspired quite a few including JumpStartFund, a Southern California startup, to do just that.

Elon Musk clearly is one of the top innovators and visionaries of our time!

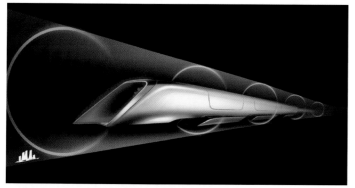

# A New Way to Buy

Tesla is reinventing how cars are purchased. First, Tesla sells its cars directly over the Internet. And Tesla's company-owned showrooms differ greatly from the traditional franchise dealerships. These showrooms are purposefully located in popular high-end shopping mall areas because their primary purpose is not to book orders. Instead, Tesla measures showroom success on how well they enlighten a potential car buyer on the experience and lifestyle of driving an electric car, in particular a Tesla Model S. This is where customers view cars, get test drives, and have questions answered by the non-commissioned Product Specialists.

This pleasant, educational environment is similar to the customer experience found at Apple Stores. This is not surprising since George Blankenship, Vice President Sales and Ownership Experience at Tesla Motors was Vice President, Real Estate for Apple Computer. Under his leadership, Tesla's first-of-its-kind car retail approach avoids back-room games, "buy right-now" pressure tactics, and bundled expensive add-ons you don't need or want. At Tesla, you buy when you are ready and everyone pays the same price, so there's no haggling to get the price down from some artificially high price.

Cars are also built to order, so you get exactly what you want. Tesla's friendly approach actually makes purchasing a car fun!

*George Blankenship*

# Dealers vs. Consumers

Tesla's ground breaking sales approach of selling directly to the consumer is upsetting conventional car dealers. Tesla elected to bypass the dealer network sales and service approach and sells its cars built-to-order online over the Internet. Tesla showrooms offer a no-pressure introduction to the cars. Non-commissioned associates are there to educate, not sell.

Selling through existing dealerships does not make sense for Tesla or its customers. The Model S is built-to-order avoiding the need to sit on a dealer's car lot. Since EVs are new to most consumers, Tesla needs a dedicated showroom, not a dealership selling competing brands and models besides Tesla's cars. Tesla is a high tech car company dedicated to making great products at increasingly lower prices. Dealers often tack on all sorts of imaginative costs such as advertising fee, delivery fee, protection fees, employee party fee, etc. The dealer markup also results in a significant higher cost to the consumer. Just the opposite of what Tesla is trying to achieve.

Surprisingly, dealers make most of their profits from service and parts – both warranty and after warranty work. It's obvious why dealers don't want to sell a reliable car like the Model S that requires minimal servicing. Dealers have an inherent conflict of interest. The dealer makes more money in service with a unreliable car.

The dealers are fighting tooth-and-nail to prevent Tesla from selling cars to consumers. State franchise laws enacted in the 1920s make little sense today. They were

### Legal Victory
Tesla won the lawsuit brought by the Massachusetts Auto Dealers Association who tried to stop Tesla sales in that state.

a major contributing factor in the bankruptcy of GM and Chrysler.

Over the objections of consumers, some state legislatures have succumbed to the extreme pressure of powerful dealer association lobbyists. In Texas, Tesla is not even allowed to tell the consumer the price of the car! The Texas consumer has to visit Tesla's website to learn the price.

North Carolina is trying to prevent Tesla from even selling online. Consumers overwhelmingly want the right to buy what they want, when and how they want. Many want to avoid the painful, dreaded "dealer experience". Auto Dealers might be wise to tone down their protectionist tactics. They may ignite a public backlash and lose a lot more than just a few car sales.

# Marketing

Tesla's Marketing Strategy is as pioneering and innovative as its Model S sports sedan. Instead of paying for traditional automotive marketing promotions, such as expensive television and print ads, Tesla is building its brand awareness through social media, special events, word of mouth, and positive experience when customers visit their company-owned stores located in upscale shopping malls.

Tesla has received numerous and extremely positive reviews by getting the car in the hands of key car reviewers. A reviewer for the San Jose Mercury News was given a Model S for a weekend. Not only was she smitten but so was her son. This strategy can be risky, as there is no control over what's written. Fortunately, the Model S exceeds expectations and the press continues to be wowed!

To keep the spotlight on the Model S, Tesla continues to release major announcements that excite customers. Elon Musk effectively uses blogs and tweets to build interest in upcoming corporate announcements, or to respond quickly to any misconceptions or inaccuracies. Tesla gets plenty of free positive press using social media as it pumps out breakthrough announcements, such as:

- Free long distance fuel for the life of the car
- Super fast 20 minute charging for 150 miles of range
- Battery swap system takes less time than a gas fill up
- Model S received highest overall vehicle safety score
- Superchargers to go nationwide
- New lower-cost sedan and SUV for 2018

This has clearly been a winning strategy for Tesla and continues to build customer awareness.

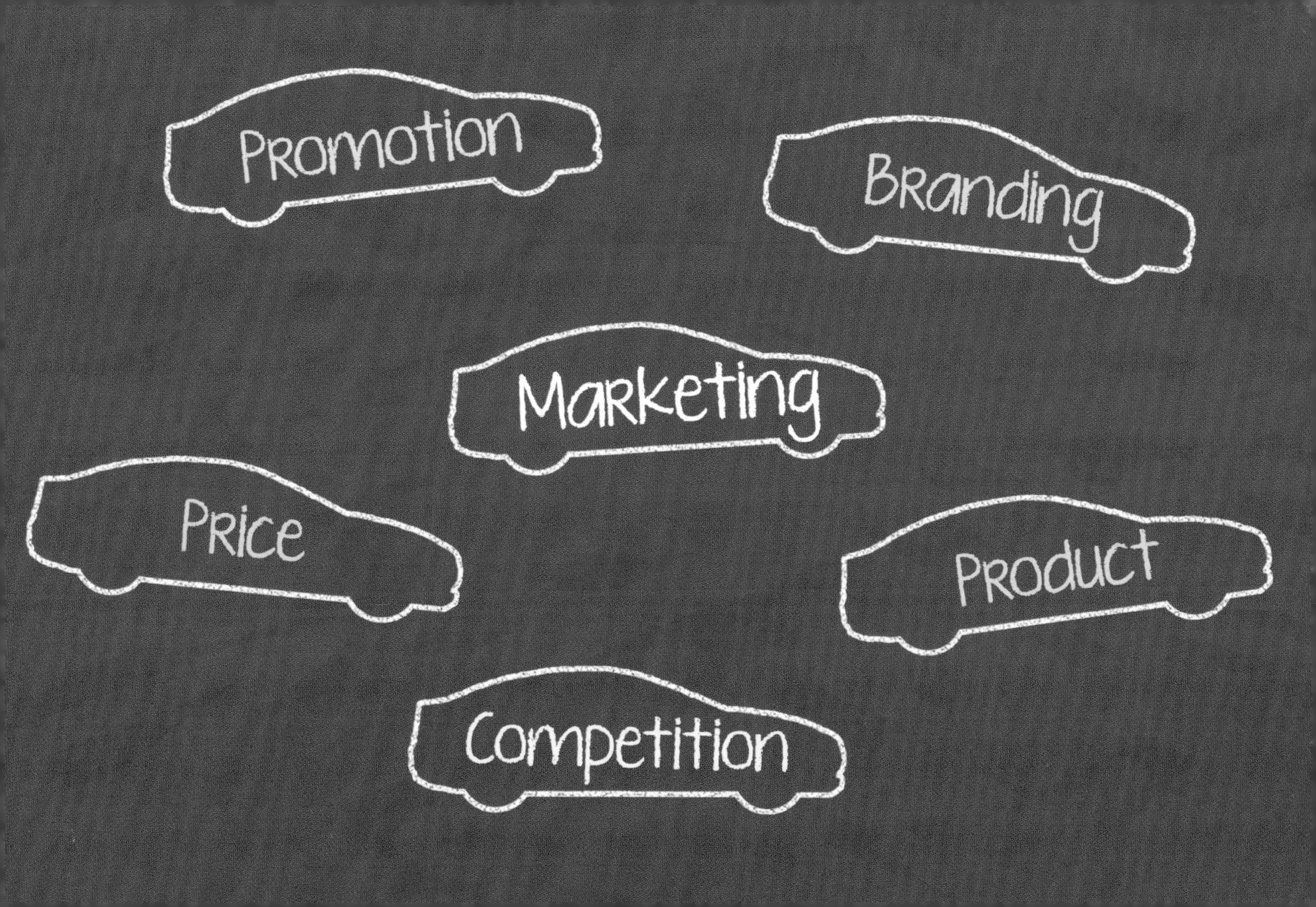
Promotion
Branding
Marketing
Price
Product
Competition

# Subsidies for Everyone

Many countries around the world offer subsidies, rebates or reduced taxes for consumers who purchase a new non-polluting vehicle like the Model S. Even China offers rebates up to 60,000 yuan, (approximately US $9700) towards the purchase of an electric car.

In the USA, the federal government offers a $7500 tax credit for electric vehicles like the Model S. Many states also offer additional subsidies and rebates that range from $750 to $7500. The primary objective of these subsides is to reduce the dependence on oil, spur new technologies, and reduce pollution. The combined US federal and state subsidies amount to less than 400 million dollars a year for consumers.

In a country like Norway, the price differences are extreme. A new BMW M5 that costs $90,000 in the USA costs $280,000 in Norway after VAT and import taxes.

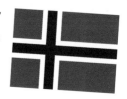

The Model S is exempt from both VAT and import tax, so the cost is about the same as USA pricing before US tax credits. In addition, the yearly $500 road fee is waived.

People criticize the electric car subsidies and incentives but every energy industry and transport system in USA gets subsidies. Key to the development of USA, railroads were one of the first supported by public funding. Amtrak still gets a significant subsidy today. Funds for building local airports come primarily from the FAA budget. In 2013 alone, the FAA allocated $2.5 billion for airport safety improvements.

### Cool Fact
West Virginia gives the largest state subsidy in the USA, $7500 per qualifying EV car.

The oil, gas and coal industries enjoy subsidies and tax breaks too. From 1918 to today, the federal government gave the oil and gas industry over $450 billion (adjusted for inflation) in energy subsidies. While it's hard to get an exact number, current oil, gas, and coal subsidy estimates in the USA range from 10 to 52 billion dollars a year.

Many attempts to eliminate these subsidies have failed due to the very successful efforts of the fossil fuel lobby. The International Energy Agency estimates that global tax subsidies for fossil fuels exceed $500 billion just in 2011 alone!

## US Government Technologies Loan

The Department of Energy's Advanced Technologies Vehicles Manufacturing loan program has been often incorrectly identified as a subsidy. This is a loan that is secured by stock and assets of the receiving company. The four companies who received loans for specific projects include Ford Motor, Nissan, Tesla Motors, and Fisker Automotive. Tesla repaid the loan in full in the spring of 2013, with interest, nine years earlier than required at a profit to the government of over $20 million.

Governments around the world understand the importance of encouraging emerging technologies like electric cars and clean energy. The payoff has always been job creation, economic expansion and solving important human problems.

# Future in Motion

Tesla's future is incredibly bright and so is the future of electric vehicles. Tesla continues to innovate in four major areas: current model improvements, battery technology, Supercharger network, and launching new models.

For the Model S, Tesla keeps adding new functionality with each free software update. Tesla also continues to customize the Model S for regional markets such as a right-hand drive version for the UK, Japanese and other markets. The Chinese market demands a special luxury rear seat for chauffeur driven owners, so Tesla is making an option to accommodate this need. There's even speculation that an AWD version of the Model S may appear in the future.

Tesla anticipates that improving cell chemistry in the battery pack could eventually deliver 500 miles of range! When battery capacity improves enough, Tesla could then offer swappable battery packs if customers were willing to pay for such an upgrade.

Top on the priority list for Tesla is the build out of its Supercharger network. The popularity of the free Superchargers keeps Tesla scrambling to increase nationwide coverage in every country it sells in. Tesla is also pushing further advances in Supercharging. While swapping out battery packs has been demonstrated to work, Tesla thinks reducing charging times during long distance travel is preferable. Ultimately, CTO JB Straubel says that Tesla aims to achieve a five to ten minute maximum recharge time at a Supercharger station.

Tesla has already revealed its next vehicle, the 7-passenger sport utility vehicle, Model X. It's based on the Model S platform, and shares quite a bit of its powertrain and design. The Model X also brings many new innovations,

including the first falcon wing rear doors for easy egress to the 2nd and 3rd rows. Tesla also provides a dual-motor all-wheel drive option that should outperform the competition by a wide margin. Tesla debuted the Model X with dual video cameras in place of conventional side mirrors for reduced wind resistance. Due to state and federal regulations, it looks like they will have to go with conventional side mirrors as shown on the right.

After the Model X, comes a smaller sedan at a lower price point with 200 miles of range. It's intended to be Tesla's affordable mass-market EV. It may even have some "autopilot or self-driving element" according to Elon Musk. As of this writing, it may go under the name "Model E".

Other potential models are undoubtedly on the drawing boards. Tesla has hinted it may squeeze in a roadster style sports car as well! At the first Teslive conference, Elon Musk also imagined issues to solve should Tesla design a pickup truck.

As for the future of electric vehicles, Elon Musk optimistically predicts:

- In five years, EVs will regularly appear on the road because 100,000's of new EVs will be sold each year.

- In fifteen years, the majority of new cars built will be electric cars

- After EVs become the majority of new cars built, it will take another 10 to 12 years to replace the installed base of gas cars with electric ones.

How can EVs outnumber or even supplant ICE cars? Improving battery energy density is critical to making EVs cheaper and lighter. Already, such disruptive energy technology exists in laboratory testing. So the future of electric cars is indeed growing brighter every day.

Tesla definitely scored a winner with its Model S! Like Ford's Model T, we will look back years from now and realize it was the "car of the century," a game changer. I can't wait for the next big thing from Tesla.

# The Finish Line

By now some of you may think I work for Tesla – I don't. I also unfortunately, don't own any Tesla stock. I didn't get paid by anyone to write this and I paid the same price as everyone else for my Model S. I am a bit of a fan, but like so many owners, it's a car you can easily fall in love with. If you've skipped over everything else in this book, a few points to keep in mind about the Model S:

- Great comfort, style, and fun to drive

- Dramatically lower fuel costs, and you can fuel at home

- Free fuel for long distance travel with Superchargers

- Produces no pollution or $CO_2$ when driving

- High reliability and low maintenance – far fewer parts to break down or wear out

- No more oil and filter changes

- More cargo space than many SUVs

- Safest production car you can drive

Bonus Features for EVs:

- Preferred parking spots offered in many cities

- Smog checks are never required

- May have substantial rebates, lower taxes and fees

- Solo drivers use commuter lanes in many areas

To sum it up, the Model S really is the best car ever. I hope to see you on the road in a Model S soon!

# Links and Attributions

## Main Links

- **TeslaMotors.com** - Tesla's official company site with pricing, specifications, accessories and forum
- **TeslaMotorsClub.com** - Forum site and Teslive
- **TeslaRun.com** - Tour De Tesla's Southern California Tesla run
- **TeslaTap.com** - Our own site with features, how-to modifications, important links, and much more

## Accessories and Modifications

- **Al-Eds.com** - Products store and Tesla specific mods
- **TeslaAccessories.com** - Center console and more
- **TorkLiftCentral.com** - Trailer hitch and more
- **Tsportline.com** - Wheels, accents and mods
- **VossenWheels.com** - Wheels

## Quotes

On page 2, The Lefsetz Letter, from: http://lefsetz.com/wordpress/index.php/archives/2013/06/24/the-tesla/

On page 10, Franz von Holzhausen, from: Tesla Motors video "Introduction to the Model S".

On page 85: Elon Musk, from Tesla press release "Tesla Motors Launches Revolutionary Supercharger" on September 25, 2012.

On page 153: Elon Musk, from New York Times, April 15, 2008

On page 196, Elon Musk, from: http://green.autoblog.com/2006/07/26/exclusive-q-and-a-with-elon-musk-on-the-tesla-roadster-and-the-fut/

## Photo Attributions

Principal photography: © Frank van Gilluwe; Some photos are simulations, composited or otherwise modified for clarity and illustrative purposes. A huge thanks go out to everyone that contributed photos to this project!

# Index